LIFE OF BLACK HAWK

A NEW EDITION

Edited by

DONALD L. FIXICO

WESTHOLME
Yardley

To all People of the Sac and Fox Nations

Life of Ma-Ka-Tai-Me-She-Kia-Kiak or Black Hawk edited by J. B. Patterson first published in 1833. This edition edited and introduced by Donald L. Fixico published by Westholme in 2026.

Westholme Publishing, LLC
904 Edgewood Road
Yardley, Pennsylvania 19067
Visit our Web site at www.westholmepublishing.com

ISBN: 978-1-59416-477-4
Also available as an eBook.

Printed in the United States of America.

CONTENTS

Illustrations

MAPS

IMAGES

(An unnumbered gallery follows page 86)

INTRODUCTION

The citizens of the Sac and Fox Nation in Oklahoma are extremely proud of their famous leader—Black Hawk. Similar pride is felt by the Sac and Fox Nation of the Mississippi in Tama, Iowa, and the Sac and Fox Tribe of Kansas in Reserve, Kansas. Black Hawk is a highly revered leader, and virtually every Sac and Fox tribal member knows his name. Today, the estimated population for all three federally recognized tribes is 6,400 members. In Stroud, Oklahoma, Black Hawk's portrait hangs proudly in the administration building of the Sac and Fox Nation.

In 1833, after the Black Hawk War of 1832, Black Hawk dictated his autobiography to John B. Patterson, an Illinois newspaper editor, and Antoine Leclair, who was the US interpreter for the Sacs and Foxes. As one of the first American Indian autobiographies, this "as told to" account by an American Indian became a controversial bestseller.[1] There are only a few similar notable works: William

1. J. B. Patterson, *Life of Ma-Ka-Tai-Me-She-Kia-Kiak or Black Hawk* (Cincinnati, 1833).

Apes (Pequot), *A Son of the Forest: The Experience of William Apes, a Native of the Forest: Comprising a Notice of the Pequod tribe of Indians*, an autobiography (1829); *Geronimo's Story of His Life*, an autobiography (1906); and the renowned classic, *Black Elk Speaks: Being the Life Story of an Oglala Holyman* (1932), edited by John Neihardt.[2] Black Hawk's volume is a revealing account of the war leader's point of view regarding the protection of his people and their homeland. At times, his words seem simplistic and his views myopic, but the volume is enlightening for people of all ages. His words convey the cultural and political contexts of Indian-white relations on the frontier. Most relevant are the insights into what Black Hawk felt, what he was thinking, and the reasons behind his actions. Simultaneously, the book iterates how the Sauk warrior and his people were treated by the British and the Americans during settler expansion when other peoples of all kinds (i.e., other tribes, French, British, and Americans) wanted the homeland of the Sauk and Fox.

In the immediate years after the release of Black Hawk's autobiography in 1833, the book received criticism while garnering more attention to the elderly war leader. Newspapers discredited both the book and Black Hawk, with Black Hawk receiving increasing attention due to persisting Indian wars. In a Vandalia, Illinois, newspaper one critic said, "The facts as stated may be true, but are not worth the time and trouble which have been employed in throwing them together." He scoffed, "This work and the Life of David Crockett, ought to be placed on the same

2. William Apes, *A Son of the Forest: The Experience of William Apes, a Native of the Forest: Comprising a Notice of the Pequod tribe of Indians* (pub. by author, 1829), S. M. Barrett, ed., *Geronimo's Story of His Life* (Duffield and Company, 1906), and John Neihardt, ed., *Black Elk Speaks: Being the Life Story of an Oglala Holyman* (William Morrow and Company, 1932).

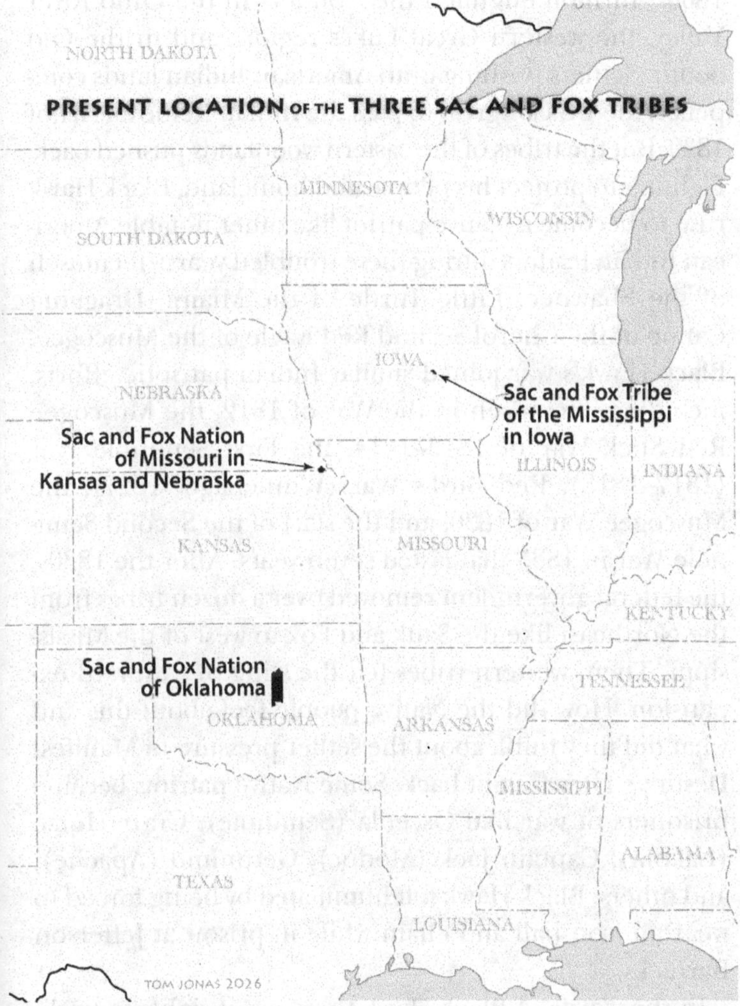
PRESENT LOCATION OF THE THREE SAC AND FOX TRIBES
NORTH DAKOTA
MINNESOTA
WISCONSIN
SOUTH DAKOTA
IOWA
NEBRASKA
Sac and Fox Tribe of the Mississippi in Iowa
Sac and Fox Nation of Missouri in Kansas and Nebraska
ILLINOIS
INDIANA
KANSAS
MISSOURI
KENTUCKY
Sac and Fox Nation of Oklahoma
TENNESSEE
OKLAHOMA
ARKANSAS
MISSISSIPPI
ALABAMA
TEXAS
LOUISIANA
TOM JONAS 2026

shelf."[3] For certain, the names Black Hawk and Davy Crockett would not be forgotten!

During Black Hawk's life in the late 1700s and early 1800s, turmoil engulfed the frontiers in the Ohio River Valley, the western Great Lakes region, and in the Old South. Settlers pushing onto American Indian lands compelled the US Congress to pass the Indian Removal Act of 1830. But the tribes of the eastern woodlands pushed back. Fighting to protect his people and homeland, Black Hawk rose to become a Native patriot like other notable American Indian leaders during these troubled years: Tecumseh of the Shawnee, Little Turtle of the Miami, Dragging Canoe of the Cherokee, and Red Eagle of the Muscogee. Black Hawk's war joined similar Indian patriotic efforts, including Tecumseh in the War of 1812, the Muscogee Red Stick War of 1813–1814, the First Seminole War (1817–1818), Red Bird's War (Winnebago, 1827), the Muscogee War of 1836, and the start of the Second Seminole War in 1835 that lasted seven years. After the 1830s, the federal government removed over a dozen tribes from the Northeast like the Sauk and Fox to west of the Mississippi. Then, western tribes felt the sting of westward expansion. How did the Native people feel about this and what did they think about the settler pressure of Manifest Destiny? They fought back. Some Native patriots became prisoners of war like Osceola (Seminole), Crazy Horse (Lakota), Captain Jack (Modoc), Geronimo (Apache), and others. Black Hawk felt humiliated by being forced to wear an iron ball and chain while in prison at Jefferson Barracks.

In the words of Black Hawk there are insights to traditional lifeways, Indigenous ethos, Sauk and Fox worldview,

3. "Life of Black Hawk," *Vandalia Whig and Illinois Intelligencer*, January 15, 1834, originally published in the *Louisville Herald.*

and American Indian reality consisting of a metaphysical and physical realm where visions, dreams, and spirits were real. In 1882, another edition of Black Hawk's autobiography was published. It contained additional sections of information, but they were not the words of the Sauk leader. However, two pertinent sections, Black Hawk's Tower and Mr. Graham's Speech, have been included in this edition.

Black Hawk's true name was Black Sparrowhawk, and he was a Sauk, later known as the Sac Tribe. In the 1730s, Black Hawk's people, the Sauks, joined with the Mesquakies, who are commonly known as the Foxes. The Sauks, also known as the Osakiwugi, were the people of the yellow earth and the Foxes, or Mesquakies, were the people of the red earth. They were once two nations but became allies in war due to much fighting in what would become western Illinois.

The Sac and Fox people had a dozen clans or more. Today, ten are active. The current clans are Fish, Ocean, Thunder, Bear, Fox, Bear Potato, Deer, Beaver, Snow, and Wolf. Black Hawk was born into the Thunder Clan by his mother, whose name was Summer Rain. By tradition, the Thunder Clan produced warriors.

From about 1712 to 1730, the Fox people fought against French expansion into the western Great Lakes in what became known as the Fox Wars. The French sought beaver pelts and the Fox saw the French coureur de bois (frontier traders) as intruders, and many of them married Fox women. After two or three councils with the Sauks, the Foxes decided to move and live next to the Sauks on the Rock River, a tributary of the Upper Mississippi River. Soon afterward, the area became known as Illinois and joined the United States in 1818. Only two years earlier, the Sauk had established Saukenuk on the north side of the Rock River below some rapids where the river joins the Mississippi River. There is no English translation for "Saukenuk," but it suggests the Sauk's true home place of at least a hundred lodges. It became the main town of the Sauk and Fox.

In the late 1700s, a powerful medicine maker of the Eagle Clan won the respect of the Sauk people. His name was Pyesa, and he was Black Hawk's father. Black Hawk's clan did not provide hereditary leaders for the Sauks. This left Black Hawk to earn recognition as a warrior by joining raids and leading attacks against their enemies, the Osage and Cherokee. Black Hawk joined his first raid when he was fifteen years old.

Black Hawk possessed a warrior's heart. Today, he is a role model, especially for Native youths and for all young people. He epitomized integrity and true patriotism in fighting for his people and establishing Sac and Fox identity. He believed people should be honest and trustworthy.

Black Hawk was born in 1767 at Saukenuk on the Rock River. As a young man, Black Hawk earned distinction as a new warrior by wounding a man in a fight against the Osages, the frequent enemy of the Sauk and Fox. In this battle, Black Hawk fought alongside his father, who witnessed his son wounding an Osage warrior. In the following years, Black Hawk had limited success in earning further recognition. It was not until he was nineteen years old that he led a successful attack of two hundred warriors against the Osage. In this conflict, Black Hawk killed five warriors and one woman.

Black Hawk faced a turning point in his young life when he joined a war party that included his father, Pyesa, against the Cherokees. In the pitch of the battle, Pyesa was wounded and soon died from his injuries. Pyesa was the keeper of the sacred Sauk and Fox medicine bundle, the metaphysical power of the people. The enormous responsibility of caring for the bundle fell to Black Hawk, who was about twenty years old at the time.

Black Hawk exuded much pride in being a Sauk. And his leadership sustained the Sauk and Fox people through challenges against enemy tribes, settlers, militia, and soldiers. He survived many engagements and won numerous victories. After feeling much wrongdoing had been inflicted upon the Sauk and Fox by white settlers, sixty-five-year-old Black Hawk decided to lead his small band, sometimes called the British band, to reclaim their beloved Saukenuk.

During these troubled times, White Cloud, the Winnebago Prophet, heavily influenced Black Hawk. In early 1832, White Cloud foretold that the British and local tribes would join Black Hawk's cause in driving the American settlers from the western Illinois area. Black Hawk listened and believed, but the prophecy did not come true.

On May 15, 1832, a force of Illinois militia attacked Black Hawk's band at Stillman's Run. The militia then retreated. In June and the first part of July, Gen. Henry Atkinson and Gen. Winfield Scott pursued Black Hawk's band through northern Illinois and into Wisconsin. On July 27, although heavily outnumbered, Black Hawk and his warriors defeated the soldiers at Wisconsin Heights. Exhausted from fighting with no time to recover, Black Hawk and his people of about one thousand (mostly women and children) were defeated badly at the two-day Battle of Bad Axe on August 1 and 2. In the following days, Black Hawk surrendered to American officials at Prairie du Chien, and the Treaty of Fort Armstrong on September 21, 1832, ended the Black Hawk War.

Six years later, in 1838, the war leader "walked west" to join his ancestors. After two weeks of suffering from a respiratory illness, the aged war leader died on October 3 at the age of seventy-one. He was buried on the north bank of the Des Moines River in southeast Iowa. Black Hawk lived a long life.

In 1882, a revised edition of the 1833 Black Hawk autobiography was published by J. B. Patterson at Oquawka, Illinois.[4] The latter edition contained five added sections: "Starts for a New Home," "Black Hawk's Last Visit," "Black Hawk's Removal to the Des Moines River," "Fox Murderers Wanted" and "The Black Hawk War," with a preface. Although not in Black Hawk's words, topics like "Stillman's Defeat," "Kilbourn's Narrative: A Reminiscence of Black Hawk," "Battle of Pecantonica," "Fight at Apple River Fort," "Apple River Fort," "Kellog's Grove Fort," "Major's Dement's Battle with the Indians," "At Wisconsin Heights," "Steamboat Warrior's Fight," and "General Atkinson's Report" of August 25, 1832, are generally brief with only several paragraphs each, but are rich in detail. An appendix of several pages follows with superfluous information for readers wanting to know the full regional context of the early 1800s leading up to the Black Hawk War of 1832.

Not too long after the 1882 edition was published, the legacy of Black Hawk began its own course in intriguing ways. In 1926, millionaire Maj. Frederick McLaughlin bought the Portland Rosebuds professional hockey team, a member of the Western Canadian Hockey League. McLaughlin moved the team to Chicago and renamed it the Blackhawks after his former 86th Infantry army division in World War I. Formed in 1917, the division was called "The Blackhawks" or "Blackhawk" due to most of

4. J. B. Patterson, *Autobiography of Ma-Ka-Tai-Me-She-Kia-Kiak or Black Hawk* (Continental Printing Company, 1882).

the soldiers coming from the states of Illinois, Wisconsin, and Minnesota, the home territory of Black Hawk.

Moline Community College in Illinois was founded in 1946 to help accommodate World War II veterans who lived in the area and wanted a college education. It was renamed Black Hawk College in 1961. Every academic year, the college averages over eight thousand students.

Throughout the United States, there are eight cities named Blackhawk: in Illinois, Wisconsin, Indiana, Iowa, Kentucky, Mississippi, Colorado, and South Dakota. Over thirty high schools have Black Hawk as their team mascot. Over a dozen parks in the United States are named Black Hawk or Blackhawk.

Due to Black Hawk's aggressive warrior spirit in battle, the Boeing Company developed the YUH-60 helicopter in October 1974. The US Army adopted an updated version of the attack helicopter and named it the Black Hawk in 1979. Afterward, a new design was developed. In October 2025, the S70UASU Hawk, the first totally autonomous Black Hawk helicopter, was made known to the public.[5]

Through various ways mentioned here, the legacy of Black Hawk, the famed war leader of the Sauk and Fox, continues. But he is much more than just a memory among Sac and Fox people. More than a legend, his spirit is among us. Black Hawk's autobiography has been edited

5. The YUH-60 Black Hawk (Y means prototype, U utility, H helicopter, and 60 is the assigned identity number); S70UASU Hawk (S70 means Sikorsky S-70 aircraft family, UAS means unmanned aircraft, and U Hawk means unmanned Black Hawk). Lockheed Martin News Releases, "Sikorsky Converts BLACK HAWK Into U-Hawk, A Battle-Ready Autonomous UAS," October 13, 2025, accessed May 20, 2026, https://news.lockheedmartin.com/2025-10-13-Sikorsky-Converts-BLACK-HAWK-into-U-Hawk-A-Battle-Ready-Autonomous-UAS.

and reproduced several times, but this is the first time it has been edited by a member of the Sac and Fox Nation, and I am of the Fox Clan. As part of that editing, I have regularized the names of the tribes mentioned in the text to their current spellings.

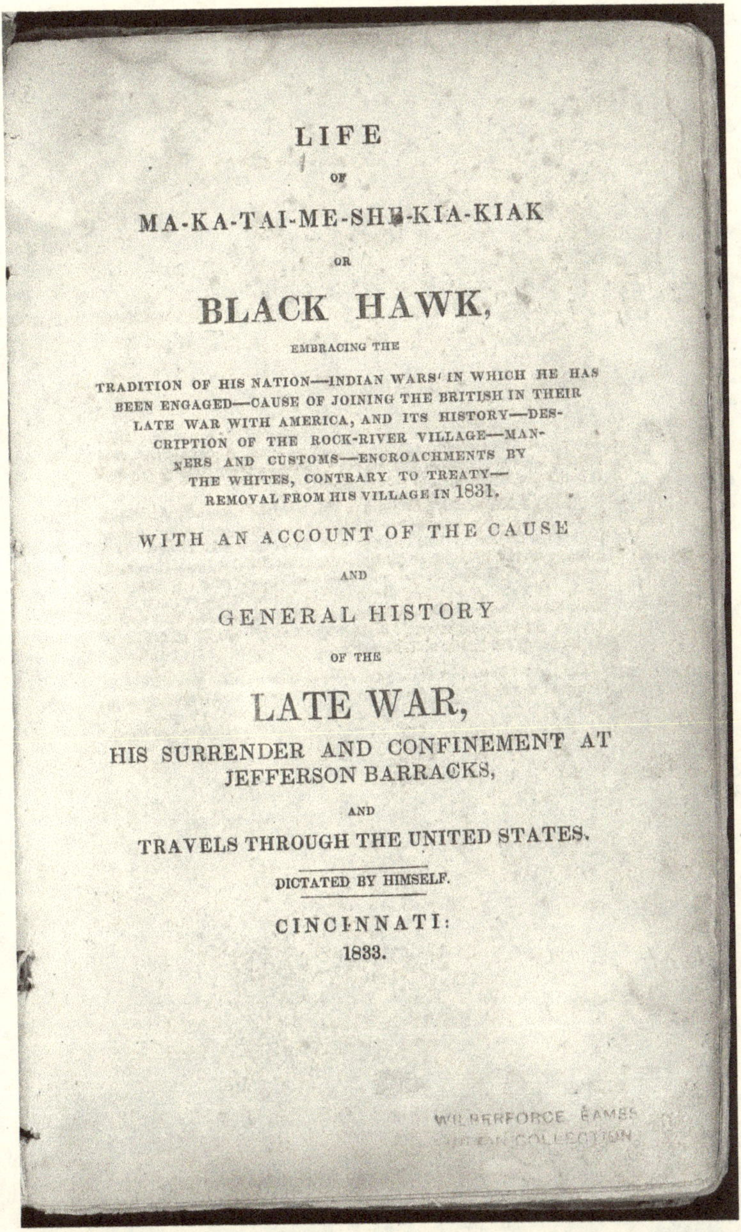

LIFE

OF

MA-KA-TAI-ME-SHE-KIA-KIAK

OR

BLACK HAWK,

EMBRACING THE

TRADITION OF HIS NATION—INDIAN WARS IN WHICH HE HAS BEEN ENGAGED—CAUSE OF JOINING THE BRITISH IN THEIR LATE WAR WITH AMERICA, AND ITS HISTORY—DESCRIPTION OF THE ROCK-RIVER VILLAGE—MANNERS AND CUSTOMS—ENCROACHMENTS BY THE WHITES, CONTRARY TO TREATY—REMOVAL FROM HIS VILLAGE IN 1831.

WITH AN ACCOUNT OF THE CAUSE

AND

GENERAL HISTORY

OF THE

LATE WAR,

HIS SURRENDER AND CONFINEMENT AT JEFFERSON BARRACKS,

AND

TRAVELS THROUGH THE UNITED STATES.

DICTATED BY HIMSELF.

CINCINNATI:

1833.

Title page of the first edition of *Life of Black Hawk.* (*New York Public Library*)

Charles Gordon Greene, Printer,
19 Water Street.

INDIAN AGENCY
Rock-Island, *October* 16, 1833.

I DO HEREBY CERTIFY, that Mà-ka-tai-me-she-kià-kiàk, or Black Hawk, did call upon me, on his return to his people in August last, and express a great desire to have a History of his Life written and published, in order, (as he said) "that the people of the United States, (among whom he had been travelling, and by whom he had been treated with great respect, friendship and hospitality,) might know the *causes* that had impelled him to act as he has done, and the *principles* by which he was governed." In accordance with his request, I acted as Interpreter; and was particularly cautious, to understand distinctly the narrative of Black Hawk throughout—and have examined the work carefully, since its completion—and have no hesitation in pronouncing it strictly correct, in all its particulars.

Given under my hand, at the Sac and Fox Agency, the day and date above written.

ANTOINE LECLAIR,
U.S. Interpreter for the Sacs and Foxes.

NE-KA-NA-WEN.

MA-NE-SE-NO O-MAUT WAP-PI MA-QUAI.

WA-TA-SAI WE-YEU,

Ai nan-ni ta co-si-ya-quai, na-katch ai she-ke she-he-nack, hai-me-ka-ti ya-quai ke-she-he-nack, ken-e-cha we-he-ke kai-pec-kien a-cob, ai we-ne-she we-he-yen; ne-wai-ta-sa-mak ke-kosh-pe kai-a-poi qui-wat. No-ta-wach-pai pai-ke se-na-mon nan-ni-yoo, ai-ke-kai na-o-pen. Ni-me-to sai-ne-niwen, ne-ta-tota ken ai mo-he-man tà-ta-que, ne-me-to-sai-ne-ne-wen.

Nin- àk ài-ka poi-pon-ni chii-cha-yen, kai kà-ya ha-ma-we pa-she-to-he-yen. Kài-na-ya kai-nen-ne-naip, he-nok ki-nok ke-chà-kai-ya, pai-no-yen ne-ket-te-sim-mak o-ke-te- wak ke-o-che, me-ka ti-yaquois na-kach mai-quoi, à-que-qui pà-che-qui ke-kan-ni tà-men-nin. Ke-to-tà we-yen, à-que-kà-ni-cote she-tai-hai yen-nen, chai-chà-me-co kai- ke-me-se ai we-ke ken-ne-tà-mo-wàt, ken-na-wà-ha-o mà-co-quà-yeai-quoi. Ken-wen-na àk-che-màn wen-ni-ta-hài ke-men-ne to-tà-we-yeu, ke-kog-hài ke-ta-shi ke-kài nà-we-yen, he-na-cha wài-che-we to-mo-nan, ai pe-che-quà-chi mo-pen mà-me-co, mài-che-we-tà nà-mo-nan, ne-ya-we-nan qui-a-hà-wa pe-ta-kek, a que-yeàr tak-pa-she-qui à-to-tà-mo-wat, chi-ye-tuk he-ne cha-wai-chi he-ni-nan ke-o-chi-tà mow-tà-swee-pài che-quà-que.

He-ni-cha-hài poi-kài-nen nà-na-so-si-yen, ai o-sà-ke-we-yen, ke-pe-me-kai-mi-kat hài-nen hac-yài na-na-co-si-peu, nen-à-kàii-ne-co-ten ne-co-ten ne-ka chi-a-quoi ne-me-cok me-to-sai ne-ne wak-kài ne-we-yen-nen, kài-shài mà-ni-to-ke ka-to-me-nak ke-wa-sài he-co-wai mi-à-me kà-chi pài-ko-tài-hear-pe kài-cee wà-wà-kià he-pe hà-pe-nach-he-chà, na-na-ke.nà-way nitaain ai we-pa-he-weà to-to-nà, na-na-ke.nà-way ni-taain ai we-pa-he-weà to-to-nà cà, ke-to-ta-weyeak, he-nok mià-ni ai she-ke-tà ma-ke-si-yen, nen-a-kai nà-co-ten ne-ka-he-nen é-ta-quois, wà-toi-na-ka che-mà-ke-keu nà-ta-cche tài-hài-ken ai mo-co-man ye-we-yeu ke-to-towé. E-nok mà-ni-hài she-ka-tà-ma ka-siyen, wen-e-cha-hài nài-ne-mak, mài-ko-ten ke-kà-cha mà-men-na-tuk we-yowé, keu-ke-nok ai she-me ma-nà-ni tà-men-ke-yowé.

MA-KA-TAI-ME-SHE-KIA-MIAK
Ma-tàus-we Ki-sis, 1833

[TRANSLATION.]

DEDICATION.

TO BRIGADIER GEN'L H. ATKINSON.

SIR,—The changes of fortune, and vicissitudes of war, made you my conqueror. When my last resources were exhausted, my warriors worn down with long and toilsome marches, we yielded, and I became your prisoner.

The story of my life is told in the following pages; it is intimately connected, and in some measure, identified with a part of the history of your own: I have therefore, dedicated it to you.

The changes of many summers, have brought old age upon me,—and I cannot expect to survive many moons. Before I set out on my journey to the land of my fathers, I have determined to give my motives and reasons for my former hostilities to the whites, and to vindicate my character from misrepresentation. The kindness I received from you whilst a prisoner of war, assures me that you will vouch for the facts contained in my narrative, so far as they came under your observation.

I am now an obscure member of a nation, which formerly honored and respected my opinions. The path to glory is rough, and many gloomy hours obscure it. May the Great Spirit shed light on yours—and that you may never experience the humility that the power of the American government has reduced me to, is the wish of him, who, in his native forests, was once as proud and bold as yourself.

BLACK HAWK
10th Moon, 1833.

ADVERTISEMENT.

IT IS presumed no apology will be required for presenting to the public, the life of a Hero who has lately taken such high rank among the distinguished individuals of America. In the following pages he will be seen in the characters of a Warrior, a Patriot and a State-prisoner—in every situation he is still the Chief of his Band, asserting their rights with dignity, firmness and courage. Several accounts of the late war having been published, in which he thinks justice is not done to himself or nation, he determined to make known to the world, the injuries his people have received from the whites—the causes which brought on the war on the part of his nation, and a general history of it throughout the campaign. In his opinion, this is the only method now left him, to rescue his little Band—the remnant of those who fought bravely with him—from the effects of the statements that have already gone forth.

The facts which he states, respecting the Treaty of 1804, in virtue of the provisions of which Government claimed the country in dispute, and enforced its arguments with the sword, are worthy of attention. It purported to cede to the United States, all the country, including the village and corn-fields of Black Hawk and his band, on the east side of the Mississippi. Four individuals of the tribe, who were on a visit to St. Louis to obtain the liberation of one of their people from prison, were prevailed upon, (says Black Hawk,) to make this important treaty, without the knowledge or authority of the tribes, or nation.

In treating with the Indians for their country, it has always been customary to assemble the whole nation; because, as has been truly suggested by the Secretary of War, the nature of the authority of the chiefs of a tribe is such, that it is not often that they dare make a treaty of much consequence,—and we might add, never, when involving so much magnitude as the one under consideration, without the presence of their young men. A rule so reasonable and just ought never to be violated—and the Indians might well question the right of Government to dispossess them, when such violation was made the basis of its right.

The Editor has written this work according to the dictation of Black Hawk, through the United States' Interpreter, at the Sac and Fox Agency of Rock Island. He does not, therefore, consider himself responsible for any of the facts, or views, contained in it—and leaves the old Chief and his story with the public, whilst he neither asks, nor expects, any fame for his services as an amanuensis.

THE EDITOR

LIFE OF BLACK HAWK

I was born at the Sac Village, on the Rock river, in the year 1767, and am now in my 67th year.[1] My great grandfather, Na-nà-ma-kee, or Thunder, (according to the tradition given me by my father, Py-e-sa) was born in the vicinity of Montreal, where the Great Spirit first placed the Sac Nation and inspired him with a belief that, at the end of four years, he should see a *white man*, who would be to him a father.[2] Consequently he blacked his face, and eat but once a day, (just as the sun was going down,) for three years, and continued dreaming throughout all this

1. Black Hawk was born at Saukenuk, the main village of the Sauk (Sac) and Mesquakie (Fox) located on the north side of the Rock River below some rapids, and "on a broad point of land" between the river and the Mississippi River. Roger Nichols, *Black Hawk and the Warrior's Path* (Wiley-Blackwell, 1991), 7. Donald Jackson noted that Saukenuk was badly burned by George Rogers Clark in 1780 and that Illinois militiamen burned the village in 1831. Donald Jackson, ed., *Black Hawk: An Autobiography* (University of Illinois Press, 1955), 41.
2. Early Frenchmen called the Sauk "Saki" in about 1670. It was translated into English as Saukies and shortened to Sauk and Sac. Charles Callender, "Sauk," in *Handbook of North American Indians: Northeast*, vol. 15, ed. Bruce G. Trigger (Smithsonian Institution, 1978), 648–55.

time whenever he slept;—when the Great Spirit again appeared to him, and told him, that, at the end of one year more, he should meet his father,—and directed him to start seven days before its expiration, and take with him his two brothers, *Nà-mah*, or Sturgeon, and *Pau-ka-hum-ma-wa* or Sun Fish, and travel in a direction to the left of sun-rising.[3] After pursuing this course five days, he sent out his two brothers to listen if they could hear a noise, and if so, to fasten some grass to the end of a pole, erect it, pointing in the direction of the sound, and then return to him.

Early next morning they returned, and reported that they had heard sounds which appeared near at hand, and that they had fulfilled his order. They all then started for the place where the pole had been erected; when, on reaching it, Na-nà-ma-kee left his party, and went alone, to the place from whence the sounds proceeded, and found that the white man had arrived and pitched his tent. When he came in sight, his father came out to meet him.[4] He took him by the hand, and welcomed him into his tent. He told him that he was the son of the King of France—that he had been dreaming for four years—that the Great Spirit had directed him to come here, where he should meet a nation of people who had never yet seen a white man—that they should be his children, and he should be their father—that he had communicated these things to the King, his father, who laughed at him, and called him a Ma-she-na—but he insisted on coming here to meet his children, where the Great Spirit had directed

3. They were traveling west.
4. Possibly, the Frenchman was René-Robert Cavelier, Sieur de La Salle who travelled from lower Canada through the Great Lakes region and to the Mississippi River in the early 1680s.

him.[5] The King told him that he would neither find land nor people—that this was a uninhabited region of lakes and mountains; but, finding that he would have no peace without it, fitted out a nà-pe-quâ,[6] manned it, and gave it to him in charge, when he immediately loaded it, set sail, and had now landed on the very day that the Great Spirit had told him, in his dreams, he should meet his children. He had now met the man who should, in future, have charge of all the nation.[7]

He then presented him with a medal, which he hung around his neck.[8] Na-nà-ma-kee informed him of *his* dreaming,—and told him that his two brothers remained a little ways behind.[9] His father gave him a shirt, blanket, and handkerchief, besides a variety of presents, and told him to go and bring his brothers. Having laid aside his buffalo robe, and dressed himself in his new dress, he started to meet his brethren. When they met, he explained to them his meeting with the white man, and exhibited to their view the presents that he had made him—took off his medal, and placed it upon Nàh-ma, his elder brother, and requested them both to go with him to his father.

They proceeded thither,—were ushered into the tent, and, after some brief ceremony, his father opened his chest and took presents therefrom for the newcomers. He

5. "Ma-she-na" means a person not to be believed.
6. A boat.
7. Great Spirit is J. B. Patterson's understanding for the Sauk word, Gichi Manitoa.
8. The French and British strategically gave "peace medals" to Native leaders to denote which leaders were friendly in negotiations for peace and during trade relations. See Nichols, *Black Hawk,* 10.
9. Like many Native groups, the Sauk and Fox placed emphasis on dreams and dreaming as a means for revealing the future, especially the dreams of a medicine maker.

discovered that Na-nà-ma-kee had given his medal to Nàh-ma. He told him that he had done wrong—he should wear that medal himself, as he had others for his brethren: That which he had given him was a type of the rank he should hold in the nation: That his brothers could only rank as *civil* chiefs,—and their duties should consist of taking care of the village, and attending to its civil concerns—whilst his rank, from his superior knowledge, place him over them all. If the nation gets into any difficulty with another, then his puc-co-hà-wà-ma, or sovereign decree, must be obeyed. If he declared war, he must lead them on to battle: That the Great Spirit had made him a great and brave general, and had sent him here to give him that medal, and make presents to him for his people.

His father remained four days—during which time he gave him guns, powder and lead, spears and lances, and showed him their use[s];—so that in war he could chastise his enemies,—and in peace they could kill buffalo, deer, and other game, necessary for the comforts and luxuries of life. He then presented the others with various kinds of cooking utensils, and learned them their uses,—and having given them a large quantity of goods, as presents, and every other thing necessary for their comfort, he set sail for France, after promising to meet them again, at the same place, after the twelfth moon.

The three newly-made chiefs returned to their village, and explained to Muk-a-tá-quet, their father, who was the principal chief of the nation, what had been said and done. The old chief had some *dogs* killed, and made a feast, preparatory to resigning his sceptre, to which all the nation were invited.[10] Great anxiety prevailed among

10. This was a Dog Feast, a ceremonial dinner to honor individuals.

them, to know what the three brothers had seen and heard—when the old chief rose, and related to them the sayings and doings of his three sons, and concluded by observing, that "the Great Spirit had directed that these, his three children, should take the rank and power that had been his,—and that he yielded these honors and duties willingly to them,—because it was the wish of the Great Spirit, and he could never consent to make him angry!" He now presented the great medicine bag to Na-nà-ma-kee, and told him, "that he cheerfully resigned it to him—it is the soul of our nation—it has never yet been disgraced—and I will expect you to keep it unsullied!"[11]

Some dissension arose among some of them, in consequence of so much power being given to Na-nà-ma-kee, he being so young a man. To quiet this, Na-nà-ma-kee, during a violent *thunder storm*, told them that he *caused* it! and it was an exemplification of the *name* the Great Spirit had given him.[12] During this storm, the *lightning* struck, and set fire to a tree, close by; (a sight they had never witnessed before).[13] He went to it, and brought away some of its burning branches, made a fire in the lodge, and seated his brothers thereby, opposite to each other; whilst he stood up, and addressed his people as follows:

11. According to custom, the medicine bundle for the Sauk would have been made of leather from the skin of an animal and filled with certain charms, tobacco, "cedar leaves, a braid of sweetgrass, a buffalo tail amulet, a hawk skin, etc." Jackson, *Black Hawk: An Autobiography*, 49. See also, M. R. Harrington, "Sacred Bundles of the Sac and Fox Indians," *University of Pennsylvania Anthropological Publications*, 4, no. 2 (1914): 125–262.
12. With a name such as Thunder, Na-nà-ma-kee would likely have possessed the metaphysical power to cause such a thunderstorm, according to the Sauk and Fox worldview.
13. The Sauk word for "fire" is shkotêwi and "lightning bolts" is wâwâthêtonôki. Gordon Whittaker, *A Concise Dictionary of the Sauk Language* (The Sac and Fox National Public Library, 2005), 171, 191.

"I am yet young—but the Great Spirit has called me to the rank I now hold among you. I have never sought to be anything more than my birth entitled me. I have not been ambitious—nor was it ever my wish, whilst my father lives, to have taken his place—nor have I now usurped his powers. The Great Spirit caused me to dream for four years,—he told me where to go and meet the white man, who would be a kind father to us all. I obeyed his order. I went, and have seen our new father. You have all heard what was said and done. The Great Spirit directed him to come and meet me, and it is his order that places me as the head of my nation,—the place which my father has willingly resigned.

"You have all witnessed the power which has been given to me by the Great Spirit, in making that fire—and all that I now ask is, that these, my two chiefs, may never let it go out: That they preserve peace among you, and administer to the wants of the needy: And, should an enemy invade our country, I will then, but not until then, assume command, and go forth with my band of brave warriors, and endeavor to chastise them!"

At the conclusion of this speech, every voice cried out for Na-nà-ma-kee! All were satisfied, when they found that the *Great Spirit had done*, what they had suspected was the work of Na-nà-ma-kee, he being a very shrewd young man.

The next spring, according to promise, their French father returned, with his nà-pe-quâ richly laden with goods, which were distributed among them. He continued for a long time to keep up a regular trade with them—they giving him, in exchange for his goods, furs and peltries.[14]

14. The French were superb fur traders and generous with trade goods to the Sauk, Fox, and other tribes. Beaver pelts were tied into a bale that was called a "piece" and weighed about ninety pounds.

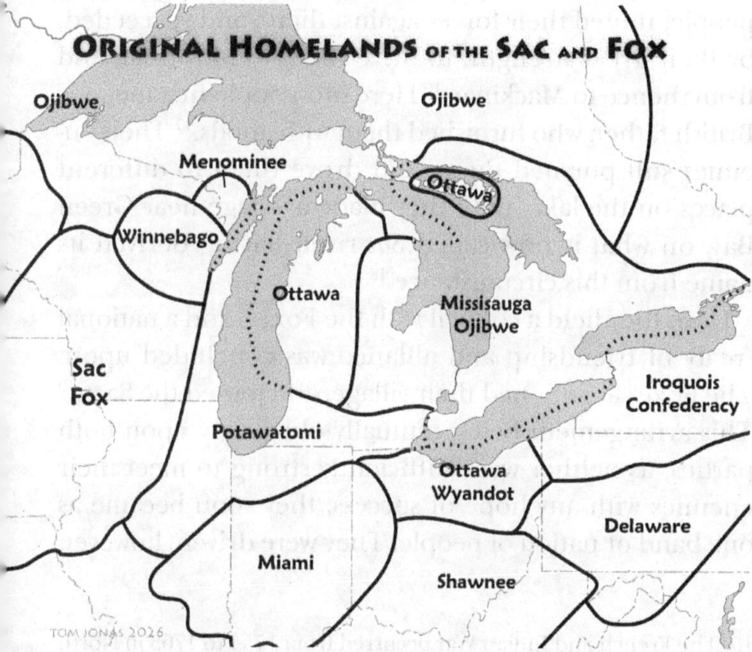
ORIGINAL HOMELANDS OF THE SAC AND FOX
Ojibwe
Ojibwe
Menominee
Ottawa
Winnebago
Ottawa
Missisauga
Ojibwe
Sac
Fox
Iroquois
Confederacy
Potawatomi
Ottawa
Wyandot
Delaware
Miami
Shawnee
TOM JONAS 2026

After a long time, the British overpowered the French, (the two nations being at war,) drove them away from Quebec, and took possession of it themselves.[15] The different tribes of Indians around our nation, envying our people, united their forces against them, and succeeded, by their great strength, to drive them to Montreal, and from thence to Mackinac.[16] Here our people first met our British father, who furnished them with goods.[17] Their enemies still pursued them, and drove them to different places on the lake, until they made a village near Green Bay, on what is now called *Sac* river, having derived its name from this circumstance.[18]

Here they held a council with the Foxes, and a national treaty of friendship and alliance was concluded upon. The Foxes abandoned their village, and joined the Sacs.[19] This arrangement being mutually obligatory upon both parties, as neither were sufficiently strong to meet their enemies with any hope of success, they soon became as one band or nation of people. They were driven, however,

15. The French and Indian War occurred from 1754 to 1763 in North America and was part the greater Seven Years' War.
16. The Mackinac area was generally the intersecting area of Lake Michigan and Lake Superior.
17. The "British father" was likely Lt. Gov. Patrick Sinclair.
18. The modern name of this river is the Fox River.
19. The Fox were also called the Meskwaki, and were known as "people of the red earth." They joined the Sauk as allies and the two tribes lived side-by-side starting in 1733 following the Second Fox War against the French. In the Second Fox War from 1728 to 1733, the French and their allied tribes, Winnebago, Cahokia, Potawatomi, Kickapoo, and the Mascouten devastated the Fox. Governor General of New France Charles de Beauharnois carried out the French design to monopolize the regional fur trade and control trade routes which the Fox tribe rejected and opposed. R. David Edmunds and Joseph L. Peyser, *The Fox Wars: The Mesquakie Challenge to New France* (University of Oklahoma Press, 1993), 133-56.

by the combined forces of their enemies, to the Wisconsin.[20] They remained here some time, until a party of their young men, (who had descended Rock river to its mouth,) returned, and made a favorable report of the country. They all descended Rock river—drove the Kas-kas-kias from the country, and commenced the erection of their village, determined never to leave it.[21]

At this village I was born, being a regular descendant of the first chief, Na-nà-ma-kee, or Thunder.[22] Few, if any, events of note, transpired within my recollection, until about my fifteenth year.[23] I was not allowed to paint, or wear feathers; but distinguished myself, at that early age, by wounding an enemy; consequently, I was placed in the ranks of the Braves!

Soon after this, a leading chief of the Mascouten nation, came to our village for recruits to go to war against the Osages, our common enemy.[24] I volunteered my services to go, as my father had joined him; and was proud to have an opportunity to prove to him that I was not an unworthy son, and that I had courage and bravery. It was not long before we met the enemy, when a battle immediately en-

20. Wisconsin River.

21. In about 1680, the Kaskaskias numbered roughly seven thousand to eight thousand. Helen Hornbeck Tanner, ed., *Atlas of Great Lakes Indian History* (University of Oklahoma Press, 1987), 5.

22. Black Hawk was born into the Thunder Clan that was known for producing warriors.

23 The transition from boyhood to manhood called for earning status as a warrior. Patrick J. Jung, *The Black Hawk War of 1832* (University of Oklahoma Press, 2007), 48.

24. The Mascouten were a tribe who originally lived along the Mississippi River near the present Wisconsin and Illinois border. The Osages lived along the Missouri River and had an estimated population of about eighteen thousand in 1800. The standard history of the Osages is John Joseph Matthews, *The Osages: Children of the Middle Waters* (University of Oklahoma Press, 1981).

sued. Standing by my father's side, I saw him kill his antagonist, and tear the scalp from his head.[25] Fired with valor and ambition, I rushed furiously upon another, smote him to the earth with my tomahawk—run my lance through his body—took off his scalp, and returned in triumph to my father! He said nothing, but looked pleased. This was the first man I killed! The enemy's loss in this engagement having been great, they immediately retreated, which put an end to the war for the present.[26] Our party then returned to our village, and danced over the scalps we had taken. This was the first time that I was permitted to join in a scalp-dance.

After a few moons had passed, (having acquired considerable fame as a *brave*,) I led a party of seven, and attacked *one hundred Osages!* I killed one man, and left him for my comrades to scalp, whilst I was taking an observation of the strength and preparations of the enemy; and, finding that they were all equally well armed with ourselves, I ordered a retreat, and came off without losing a man! This excursion gained for me great applause, and enabled me, before a great while, to raise a party of one hundred and eighty, to go against the Osages. We left our village in high spirits, and marched over a rugged country, until we reached that of the Osages, on the Missouri. We followed their trail until we arrived at their village, which we approached with great caution, expecting that they were all there; but found, to our sorrow, that they had deserted it!

25. As an act of conquering others, many tribes like the Sacs took the scalps of other Indians of enemy tribes, although scalp warfare usually refers to Indians versus whites on the frontier. William S. Kiser, *The Business of Killing Indians: Scalp Warfare and the Violent Conquest of North America* (Yale University Press, 2025), 6–7.
26. This was the Sauk-Osage Battle of 1782.

The party became dissatisfied, in consequence of this disappointment,—and all, with the exception of *five*, dispersed and returned home. I then placed myself at the head of this brave little band, and thanked the Great Spirit that *so many* remained,—and took up the trail of our enemies, with a full determination never to return without some trophy of victory! We followed on for several days—killed one man and a boy, and then returned with their scalps.

In consequence of this mutiny in my camp, I was not again enabled to raise a sufficient party to go against the Osages, until about my nineteenth year. During this interim, they committed many outrages on our nation and people. I succeeded, at length, in recruiting two hundred efficient warriors, and took up the line of march early in the morning. In a few days we were in the enemy's country, and had not travelled far before we met an equal force to contend with. A general battle immediately commenced, although my braves were considerably fatigued by forced marches. Each party fought desperately. The enemy seemed unwilling to yield the ground, and we were determined to conquer or die! A large number of the Osages were killed, and many wounded, before they commenced retreating. A band of warriors more brave, skilful, and efficient than mine, could not be found. In this engagement I killed five men and one squaw, and had the good fortune to take the scalps of all I struck, except one. The enemy's loss in this engagement was about one hundred men. Ours nineteen. We now returned to our village, well pleased with our success, and danced over the scalps we had taken.[27]

27. This was the Sauk and Fox-Osage battle of 1786 or 1787.

The Osage, in consequence of their great loss in this battle, became satisfied to remain on their own lands; and ceased, for a while, their depredations on our nation. Our attention, therefore, was directed towards an ancient enemy, who had decoyed and murdered some of our helpless women and children. I started, with my father, who took command of a small party, and proceeded against the enemy. We met near Merimack, and an action ensued; the Cherokee having greatly the advantage in numbers. Early in this engagement my father was wounded in the thigh—but had the pleasure of killing his antagonist before he fell. Seeing that he had fallen, I assumed command, and fought desperately, until the enemy commenced retreating before us. I returned to my father to administer to his necessities, but nothing could be done for him. The *medicine man* said the wound was *mortal!* from which he soon after *died!* In this battle I killed three men, and wounded several. The enemy's loss being twenty-eight, and ours seven.[28]

I now fell heir to the great *medicine bag* of my forefathers, which had belonged to my father. I took it, buried our dead, and returned with my party, all sad and sorrowful, to our village, in consequence of the loss of my father. Owing to this misfortune, I blacked my face, fasted, and prayed to the Great Spirit for five years—during which time I remained in a civil capacity, hunting and fishing.[29]

28. The Battle of Merimack, near today's Merrimac, Wisconsin, took place in about 1790 and was a Sauk and Fox victory over the Cherokees, a traditional enemy of the Sauk and Fox. This battle was in revenge for Cherokee attacks on the Sauk and Fox.
29. The Sac and Fox believe that when a person dies, the spirit walks westward where the sun goes down. A dinner feast is held for the dead by custom, and a person of about the same age and gender is adopted by the family who lost their loved one. The adopted person is given a new set of clothes and becomes a part of the family.

The Osage having commenced aggressions on our people, and the Great Spirit having taken pity on me, I took a small party and went against the enemy, but could only find *six* men! Their forces being so weak, I thought it cowardly to kill them,—but took them prisoners, and carried them to our Spanish father at St. Louis, and gave them up to him; and then returned to our village.[30] Determined on the final extermination of the Osage, for the injuries [to] our nation and people had received from them, I commenced recruiting a strong force, immediately on my return, and started, in the third moon, with five hundred Sac and Fox, and one hundred Ioway, and marched against the enemy.[31] We continued our march for several days before we came upon their trail, which was discovered late in the day. We encamped for the night; made an early start next morning, and before sun-down, fell upon *forty lodges*, and killed all their inhabitants, except *two squaws!* whom I captured and made prisoners. During this attack I killed seven men and two boys, with my own hand.[32]

In this engagement many of the bravest warriors among the Osage were killed, which caused the balance of their nation to remain on their own lands, and cease their aggressions upon our hunting grounds.

The loss of my father, by the Cherokee, made me anxious to avenge his death, by the annihilation, if possible,

30. From 1778 to 1780, the Spanish Commander at St. Louis was Fernando de Leyba.
31. The Iowa, also known as Ioway or Báxoje, lived in eastern Iowa, the state that bears their name. In 1837 they were moved from Iowa to Kansas and Nebraska until forced, once again, to Indian Territory (Oklahoma) in the late nineteenth century.
32. The Sac, Fox, and Ioway victory over the Osage was on December 10, 1805. Nichols, *Black Hawk* (Harlan Davidson, Inc., 1992), 31.

of all their race. I accordingly commenced recruiting another party to go against them. Having succeeded in this, I started, with my party, and went into their country, but only found five of their people, whom I took prisoners. I afterwards released four men—the other, a young *squaw*, we brought home. Great was my hatred for this people, I could not kill so small a party.[33]

During the close of the ninth moon, I led a large party against the Chippewa, Kaskaskia and Osage.[34] This was the commencement of a long and arduous campaign, which terminated in my thirty-fifth year; having had seven regular engagements, and a number of small skirmishes. During this campaign, several hundred of the enemy were slain. I killed *thirteen* of their bravest warriors, with my own hand.[35]

Our enemies having now been driven from our hunting grounds, with so great a loss as they sustained, we returned, in peace, to our villages; and, after the seasons of mourning and burying our dead relations, and of feast-dancing, had passed, we commenced preparations for our winter's hunt, in which we were very successful.

We generally paid a visit to St. Louis every summer; but, in consequence of the protracted war in which we had been engaged, I had not been there for some years. Our difficulties having all been settled, I concluded to take a small party, that summer, and go down to see our Spanish father. We went—and on our arrival, put up our lodges

33. The hostilities of the Sac and Fox with the Cherokees lasted from about 1790 to 1804.
34. The Chippewa, or Ojibwe, traditional homeland was across the northern Great Lakes region. They had an estimated population of about 28,000 in 1797.
35. The Sac and Fox defeat of the Chippewa, Kaskaskia, and Osage was in 1802.

where the market-house now stands. After painting and dressing, we called to see our Spanish father, and were well received. He gave us a variety of presents, and plenty of provisions. We danced through the town as usual, and its inhabitants all seemed to be well pleased. They appeared to us like brothers—and always gave us good advice.

On my next, and *last* visit to my Spanish father, I discovered, on landing, that all was not right: every countenance seemed sad and gloomy! I inquired the cause, and was informed that the Americans were coming to take possession of the town and country!—and that we should then lose our Spanish father! This news made myself and band sad—because we had always heard bad accounts of the Americans from Indians who lived near them!—and we were sorry to lose our Spanish father, who had always treated us with great friendship.[36]

A few days afterwards the Americans arrived. I took my band, and went to take leave, for the last time, of our father. The Americans came to see him also. Seeing them approach, we passed out at one door, as they entered another—and immediately started, in canoes, for our village on Rock river—not liking the change any more than our friends appeared to, at St. Louis.

On arriving at our village, we gave the news, that strange people had taken St. Louis—and that we should never see our Spanish father again! This information made all our people sorry!

Some time afterwards, a boat came up the river, with a young American chief, [Lieutenant (afterward General)

36. The United States took control of St. Louis from the Spanish on March 10, 1804, following the Louisiana Purchase of 1803, with the United States buying the Louisiana region from the French.

Pike,] and a small party of soldiers.[37] We heard of him, (by runners,) soon after he had passed Salt river. Some of our young braves watched him every day, to see what sort of people he had on board. The boat, at length, arrived at Rock river, and the young chief came on shore with his interpreter—made a speech, and gave us some presents! We, in return, presented him with meat, and such provisions as we could spare.

We were all well pleased with the speech of the young chief. He gave us good advice; said our American father would treat us well. He presented us an American flag, which was hoisted. He then requested us to pull down our *British* flags—and give him our *British medals*—promising to send us others on his return to St. Louis.[38] This we declined, as we wished to have *two Fathers!*

When the young chief started, we sent runners to the Fox village, some miles distant, to direct them to treat him well as he passed—which they did. He went to the head of the Mississippi, and then returned to St. Louis. We did not see any Americans again for some time,—being supplied with goods by British traders.

We were fortunate in not giving up our medals—for we learned afterwards, from our traders, that the chiefs high up on the Mississippi, who gave theirs, never received any in exchange for them. But the fault was not with the young American chief. He was a good man, and a great brave—and died in his country's service.

Some moons after this young chief descended the Mississippi, one of our people killed an American—and was

37. Gen. Zebulon Pike met the Sac and Fox at Saukenuk in August 1805 where he conveyed friendship from President Thomas Jefferson.
38. For more information on the history of peace medals, see Francis Paul Prucha, *Indian Peace Medals in American History* (The State Historical Society of Wisconsin, 1971).

confined, in the prison at St. Louis, for the offence. We held a council at our village to see what could be done for him,—which determined that Quàsh-quà-me, Pà-she-pa-ho, Ou-che-quà-ka, and Hà-she-quar-hí-qua, should go down to St. Louis, see our American father, and do all they could to have our friend released; by paying for the person killed—thus covering the blood, and satisfying the relations of the man murdered![39] This being the only means with us of saving a person who had killed another—and we *then* thought it was the same way with the whites!

The party started with the good wishes of the whole nation—hoping they would accomplish the object of their mission. The relatives of the prisoner blacked their faces, and fasted—hoping the Great Spirit would take pity on them, and return the husband and father to his wife and children.

Quàsh-quà-me and party remained a long time absent. They at length returned, and encamped a short distance below the village—but did not come up that day—nor did any person approach their camp! They appeared to be dressed in *fine coats* and had *medals!* From these circumstances, we were in hopes that they had brought good news. Early the next morning, the Council Lodge was crowded—Quàsh-quà-me and party came up, and gave us the following account of their mission:

"On their arrival at St. Louis, they met their American father, and explained to him their business, and urged the release of their friend. The American chief told them

39. Like many other tribes, the Sac and Fox practiced a blood tribute of making a payment in goods and often horses to the victim's family, and if the family accepted them, the misdeed was considered to be settled.

he wanted land—and they had agreed to give him some on the west side of the Mississippi, and some on the Illinois side opposite the Jeffreon.[40] When the business was all arranged, they expected to have their friend released to come home with them. But about the time they were ready to start, their friend was let out of prison, who ran a short distance, and was *shot dead!* This is all they could recollect of what was said and done. They had been drunk the greater part of the time they were in St. Louis."

This is all myself or nation knew of the treaty of 1804. It has been explained to me since. I find, by that treaty, all our country, east of the Mississippi, and south of the Jeffreon, was ceded to the United States for *one thousand dollars* a year! I will leave it to the people of the United States to say, whether our nation was properly represented in this treaty? or whether we received a fair compensation for the extent of country ceded by those *four* individuals? I could say much about this treaty, but I will not, at this time. It has been the origin of all our difficulties.[41]

Some time after this treaty was made, a war chief, with a party of soldiers, came up in keel boats, and encamped a short distance above the head of the Des Moines rapids, and commenced cutting timber amid building houses. The news of their arrival was soon carried to all the villages—when council after council was held. We could not understand the intention, or reason, why the Americans wanted to build houses at that place—but were told that they were a party of soldiers, who had brought *great guns* with them—and looked like a *war party* of whites!

40. This is the North River, eighty-two miles long and a tributary of the Mississippi River.

41. Charles J. Kappler, ed., "Treaty with the Sauk and Foxes, 1804," in *Indian Treaties 1778–1883* (Interland Publishing Inc., 1972), 74–77.

A number of our people immediately went down to see what was doing—myself among them. On our arrival, we found they were building a *fort!*[42] The soldiers were busily engaged in cutting timber; and I observed that they took their arms with them, when they went to the woods—and the whole party acted as they would do in an enemy's country! The chiefs held a council with the officers, or head men, of the party—which I did not attend—but understood from them that the war chief had said, that they were building houses for a *trader*, who was coming there to live, and would sell us goods very cheap! and that these soldiers were to remain to keep him company! We were pleased at this information, and hoped it was all true—but we could not believe that all these buildings were intended merely for the accommodation of a trader! Being distrustful of their intentions, we were anxious for them to leave off building, and go down the river again. By this time, a considerable number of Indians had arrived, to see what was doing. I discovered that the whites were alarmed!

Some of our young men watched a party of soldiers, who went out to work, carrying their arms—which were laid aside, before they commenced. Having stole up quietly to the spot, they seized the guns and gave a yell! The party threw down their axes, and ran for their arms, but found them gone! and themselves surrounded! Our young men laughed at them, and returned them their guns.

When this party came to the fort, they reported what had been done, and the war chief made a *serious* affair of it. He called our chiefs to council, inside of his fort. This

42. Old Fort Madison was built near the Des Moines River rapids.

created considerable excitement in our camp—every one wanted to know what was going to be done—and the picketing which had been put up, being low—every Indian crowded round the fort, and got upon blocks of wood, and old barrels, that they might see what was going on inside. Some were armed with guns, and others with bows and arrows. We used this precaution, seeing that the soldiers had their guns loaded—and having seen them load their *big gun* that morning!

A party of our braves commenced dancing, and proceeded up to the gate, with an intention of going in, but were stopped. The council immediately broke up—the soldiers, with their arms in their hands, rushed out of their rooms, where they had been concealed—the cannon was hauled in front of the gateway—and a soldier came running with fire in his hand, ready to apply the match. Our braves gave way, and all retired to the camp.

There was no preconcerted plan to attack the whites at that time—but I am of opinion now, had our party got into the fort, all the whites would have been killed—as the British soldiers had been at Mackinac many years before.[43]

We broke up our camp, and returned to Rock river. A short time afterwards, the fort party received a reinforcement—among whom we observed some of our old friends from St. Louis.

Soon after our return from fort Madison, runners came to our village from the *Shawnee Prophet* (whilst others were dispatched by him to the villages of the Winnebago,) with

43. On June 2, 1763, during Pontiac's Uprising, Fort Michilimackinac, later known as Fort Mackinac, was attacked and most of its British garrison was killed by Ojibwe warriors. The Ojibwe encouraged the British to open the gates of the fort prior to the attack by inviting them to watch them play baaga'adowewin, a similar game to lacrosse.

invitations for us to meet him on the Wabash.[44] Accordingly a party went from each village.

All of our party returned, among whom came a *Prophet,* who explained to us the bad treatment the different nations of Indians had received from the Americans, by giving them a few presents, and taking their land from them. I remember well his saying,—"*If you do not join your friends on the Wabash, the Americans will take this very village from you!*" I little thought, then, that his words would come true! Supposing that he used these arguments merely to encourage us to join him, we agreed that we would not. He then returned to the Wabash, where a party of Winnebago had arrived, and preparations were making for war! A battle soon ensued, in which several Winnebago were killed.[45] As soon as their nation heard of this battle, and that some of their people had been killed, they started war parties in different directions. One to the mining country; one to Prairie du Chien, and another to fort Madison. This last returned by our village, and exhibited several *scalps* which they had taken. Their success induced several other parties to go against the fort. Myself and several of my band joined the last party, and were determined to take the fort.[46] We arrived in the vicinity during the night. The spies that we had sent out several days be-

44. Tecumseh, the Shawnee war leader, and his brother, Tenskwatawa, the Shawnee Prophet, established Prophetstown in 1808 along the Wabash River in Indiana Territory. (Indiana became a state in 1816.) During these years, the Winnebago numbered roughly 1,500 in population. Tanner, *Atlas* (University of Oklahoma Press, 1987), 66.
45. This was the Battle of Tippecanoe, William Henry Harrison's defeat of Prophetstown on November 7, 1811. Tecumseh was away in the South recruiting more warriors for his cause when the battle occurred.
46. Fort Madison was located near the mouth of the Des Moines River in Iowa.

fore, to watch the movements of those at the garrison, and ascertain their numbers, came to us, and gave the following information:—"That a keelboat had arrived from below that evening, with seventeen men; that there were about fifty men in the fort, and that they marched out every morning at sunrise, to exercise."

It was immediately determined that we should take a position as near as we could, (to conceal ourselves,) to the place where the soldiers would come; and when the signal was given, each man to fire, and then rush into the fort. I dug a hole with my knife, deep enough (by placing a few weeds around it,) to conceal myself. I was so near to the fort that I could hear the sentinel walking. By daybreak, I had finished my work, and was anxiously awaiting the rising of the sun. The drum beat; I examined the priming of my gun, and eagerly watched for the gate to open. It did open—but instead of the troops marching out, a young man came alone. The gate closed after him. He passed close by me—so near that I could have killed him with my knife, but I let him pass. He kept the path towards the river; and had he went one step out of it, he must have come upon us, and would have been killed. He returned immediately, and entered the gate. I would now have rushed for the gate, and entered it with him, but I feared that our party was not prepared to follow me.

The gate opened again—four men came out, and went down to the river after wood. Whilst they were gone, another man came out, and walked towards the river—was fired upon and *killed* by a Winnebago. The others immediately ran for the fort, and two of them were killed. We then took shelter under the bank out of reach of fire from the fort.

The firing now commenced from both parties and continued all day. I advised our party to set fire to the fort, and commenced preparing arrows for that purpose. At night we made the attempt, and succeeded to fire the buildings several times, but without effect, as the fire was always instantly extinguished.[47]

The next day I took my rifle, and shot in two the cord by which they hoisted their flag, and prevented them from raising it again. We continued firing until all our ammunition was expended; and finding that we could not take the fort, returned home, having had one Winnebago killed, and one wounded, during the siege. I have since learned that the trader, who lived in the fort, wounded the Winnebago when he was *scalping* the first man that was killed! The Winnebago recovered, is now living, and is very friendly disposed towards the trader, believing him to be a *great brave!*

Soon after our return home, news reached us that a war was going to take place between the British and the Americans.[48] Runners continued to arrive from different tribes, all confirming the report of the expected war. The British agent, Col. Dixon, was holding *talks* with, and making presents to, the different tribes.[49] I had not made up my mind whether to join the British or remain neutral. *I had not discovered one good trait in the character of the Americans that had come to the country!* They made *fair promises*, but *never fulfilled them!* Whilst the *British* made but few—but we could always *rely upon their word!*

One of our people having killed a Frenchman at Prairie du Chien, the British took him prisoner, and said they would *shoot him* the next day! His family were encamped

47. This was the siege of Fort Harrison in Indiana Territory during September 1812.
48. The War of 1812.
49. Col. Robert Dickson. The British agent's last name is spelled Dixon repeatedly in the original text.

a short distance below the mouth of the Wisconsin. He begged for permission to go and see them that night, as he was *to die the next day!* They permitted him to go, after promising to return the next morning by sunrise. He visited his family, which consisted of a wife and six children. I cannot describe their *meeting* and *parting*, to be understood by the whites; as it appears that their feelings are acted upon by certain rules laid down by their *preachers!*—whilst ours are governed only by the monitor within us. He parted from his wife and children, hurried through the prairie to the fort, and arrived in time! The soldiers were ready, and immediately marched out *and shot him down!* I visited his family, and by hunting and fishing, provided for them until they reached their relations.

Why did the Great Spirit ever send the whites to this island, to drive us from our homes, and introduce among us *poisonous liquors, disease and death?* They should have remained on the island where the Great Spirit first placed them.[50] But I will proceed with my story. My memory, however, is not very good, since my late visit to the white people. I have still a buzzing in my ears, from the noise—and may give some parts of my story out of place; but I will endeavor to be correct.

Several of our chiefs and head men were called upon to go to Washington, to see their Great Father. They started; and during their absence, I went to Peoria, on the Illinois river, to see an old friend, a trader, to get his advice.[51] He was a man that always told us the truth, and knew every thing that was going on. When I arrived at Peoria, he was not there, but had gone to Chicago. I vis-

50. Saukenuk was located on Rock Island, a 17.5 square mile island at the confluence of the Rock and Mississippi Rivers.

51. Thomas Forsyth served as a subagent and later an Indian agent at Fort Armstrong on Rock Island, Illinois.

ited the Potawatomi villages, and then returned to Rock river.[52] Soon after which, our friends returned from their visit to our Great Father—and related what had been said and done. Their Great Father (they said) wished us, in the event of a war taking place with England, not to interfere on either side—but to remain neutral. He did not want our help—but wished us to hunt and support our families, and live in peace. He said that British traders would not be permitted to come on the Mississippi, to furnish us with goods—but we would be well supplied by an American trader. Our chiefs then told him that the *British traders* always gave us *credits* in the fall, for guns, powder and goods, to enable us to hunt, and clothe our families. He replied that the trader at fort Madison would have plenty of goods—that we should go there in the fall, and he would supply us on *credit,* as the *British traders had done.* The party gave a good account of what they had seen, and the kind treatment they received.

This information pleased us all very much. We all agreed to follow our Great Father's advice, and not interfere with the war. Our women were much pleased at this good news. Every thing went on cheerfully in our village. We resumed our pastimes of playing ball, horse racing, and dancing, which had been laid aside when this great war was first talked about.[53]

We had fine crops of corn, which were now ripe—and our women were engaged in gathering it, and making

52. In the late 1700s, the Potawatomi had an estimated two thousand people, Tanner, *Atlas,* 66.

53. Black Hawk's mention of playing ball was lacrosse, "the stick," likely named by French Jesuit missionary Jean de Brébeuf, who described the game in 1636 or 1637 when he saw the game being played by Huron Indians. See Donald M. Fisher, *Lacrosse: A History of the Game* (Johns Hopkins University Press, 2011).

caches to contain it. In a short time we were ready to start to fort Madison, to get our supply of goods, that we might proceed to our hunting grounds. We passed merrily down the river—all in high spirits. I had determined to spend the winter at my old favorite hunting ground, on Skunk river, and left part of my corn and mats at its mouth, to take up when I returned: others did the same. Next morning we arrived at the fort, and made our encampment. Myself and principal men paid a visit to the war chief at the fort. He received us kindly, and gave us some tobacco, pipes and provision. The trader came in, and we all rose and shook hands with him—for on him all our dependence was placed, to enable us to hunt, and thereby support our families. We waited a long time, expecting the trader would tell us that he had orders from our Great Father to supply us with goods—but he said nothing on the subject. I got up, and told him, in a short speech, what we had come for—and hoped he had plenty of goods to supply us—and told him that he should be well paid in the spring—and concluded, by informing him, that we had determined to follow our Great Father's advice, and not go to war.

He said that he was happy to hear that we intended to remain at peace. That he had a large quantity of goods; and that, if we made a good hunt, we would be well supplied: but remarked, that *he had received no instructions to furnish us any thing on credit!—nor could he give us any without receiving the pay for them on the spot!*

We informed him what our Great Father had told our chiefs at Washington—and contended that he could supply us if he would—believing that our *Great Father always spoke the truth!* But the war chief said that the trader could not furnish us on credit—and that he *had received no instructions from our Great Father at Washington!* We left the fort dissatisfied, and went to our camp. What was now to be done, we knew not. We questioned the party that brought us the news from our Great Father, that we would get credit for our winter's supplies, at this place. They still told the same story, and insisted upon its truth. Few of us slept that night— all was gloom and discontent!

In the morning, a canoe was seen descending the river—it soon arrived, bearing an express, who brought intelligence that La Gutrie, a *British trader*, had landed at Rock Island, with *two boats* loaded with goods—and requested us to come up immediately—because he had *good news* for us and *a variety of presents.*[54] The express presented us with tobacco, pipes and wampum.

The news ran through our camp like *fire in the prairie.* Our lodges were soon taken down, and all started for Rock Island. Here ended all hopes of our remaining at peace—having been *forced into* WAR *by being* DECEIVED![55]

Our party were not long in getting to Rock Island. When we came in sight, and saw tents pitched, we yelled, fired our guns, and commenced beating our drums. Guns were immediately fired at the island, returning our salute and a *British flag hoisted!* We landed, and were cordially received by La Gutrie—and then smoked the pipe with him! After which he made a speech to us, that had been sent by Colonel Dixon, and gave us a number of handsome presents—a large silk flag, and a keg of rum, and told us to retire—take some refreshments and rest ourselves, as he would have more to say to us on the next day.

54. The French fur trader Edward La Gouthrie (also La Gutrie, La Goutrie, or La Goterie) spoke fluent Sauk and worked with the British during the War of 1812 as an unofficial emissary.

55. Although Black Hawk wanted to avoid the white man's war (the War of 1812), the surrounding tribes pressured the Sauks and Foxes in joining the British as allied tribes. Nichols, *Black Hawk*, 46.

We, accordingly, retired to our lodges, (which had been put up in the mean time,) and spent the night. The next morning we called upon him, and told him that we wanted his two boats' load of goods to divide among our people—for which he should be well paid in the spring with furs and peltries. He consented—told us to take them—and do as we pleased with them. Whilst our people were dividing the goods, he took me aside, and informed me that Col. Dixon was at Green Bay, with twelve boats, loaded with goods, guns, and ammunition—and wished me to raise a party immediately and go to him. He said that our friend, the trader at Peoria, was collecting the Potawatomi, and would be there before us. I communicated this information to my braves, and a party of two hundred warriors were soon collected and ready to depart.

I paid a visit to the lodge of an old friend, who had been the comrade of my youth, and had been in many war parties with me, but was now crippled, and no longer able to travel. He had a son that I had adopted as my own, who had hunted with me the two preceding winters. I wished my old friend to let him go with me. He objected, saying that he could not get his support if his son left him: that I, (who had always provided for him since he got lame,) would be gone, and he had no other dependence than his son. I offered to leave my son in his place—but he still refused. He said he did not like the war—he had been down the river, and had been well treated by the Americans, and could not fight against them. He had promised to winter near a white settler above Salt river, and must take his son with him. We parted. I soon concluded my arrangements, and started with my party to Green Bay. On our arrival there, we found a large encampment, and were well received by Dixon, and the war chiefs that were with him. He gave us plenty of provisions, tobacco and pipes, and said he would hold a council with us the next day.[56]

In the encampment, I found a large number of Potawatomi, Kickapoo, Ottawa and Winnebago. I visited all their camps, and found them in high spirits. They had all received new guns, ammunition, and a variety of clothing. In the evening a messenger came to me to visit Col. Dixon. I went to his tent, in which were two other war chiefs, and an interpreter. He received me with a hearty shake of the hand, and presented me to the other chiefs, who shook my hand cordially, and seemed much pleased to see me. After I was seated, Col. Dixon said: "Gen. Black Hawk, I sent for you, to explain to you what we are going to do, and the reasons that have brought us here. Our friend, La Gutrie, informs us in the letter you brought from him, what has lately taken place. You will now have to hold us fast by the hand. Your English father has found out that the Americans want to take your country from you—and has sent me and his braves to drive them back to their own country. He has, likewise, sent a large quantity of guns and ammunition—and we want all your warriors to join us."

He then placed a medal round my neck, and gave me a paper, (which I lost in the late war,) and a silk flag, saying—"You are to command all the braves that will leave here the day after to-morrow, to join our braves near Detroit."[57]

56. It was common knowledge that Native men enjoyed smoking tobacco. They, and settlers, preferred a milder type called Kinnikinnick. Tobacco was used in making offerings to spirits and often was an essential part of sacred medicine bundles. See Ralph Linton, *Use of Tobacco Among North American Indians* (Field Museum of Natural History, 1924).
57. Col. Robert Dickson probably presented Black Hawk with a King George III Peace Medal.

I told him that I was very much disappointed—as I wanted to descend the Mississippi, and make war upon the settlements. He said he had been "ordered to lay the country waste around St. Louis—that he had been a trader on the Mississippi many years—had always been kindly treated, *and could not consent to send brave men to murder women and children!* That there were no soldiers there to fight; but where he was going to send us, there were a number of soldiers: and, if we defeated them, the Mississippi country should be ours!" I was pleased with this speech; it was spoken by a *brave!*

I inquired about my old friend, the trader, at Peoria, and observed, "that I expected he would have been here before me." He shook his head, and said he "had sent express after express to him, *and had offered him large sums of money,* to come, and bring all the Potawatomi and Kickapoo with him; but he refused, saying, *your British father had not money enough to induce him to join us!* I have now laid a trap for him, I have sent *Gomo,* and a party of Indians, to take him prisoner, and bring him here alive. I expect him in a few days."[58]

The next day, arms and ammunition, tomahawks, knives, and clothing, were given to my band. We had a great feast in the evening; and the morning following, I started with about *five hundred braves,* to join the British army. The British war chief accompanied us. We passed Chicago. The fort had been evacuated by the American soldiers, who had marched for fort Wayne. They were attacked a short distance from that fort, and *defeated!*[59] They had a considerable quantity of powder in the fort at Chicago, which they had *promised to the Indians;* but the

58. Gomo was a Potawatomi chief and good friend of Black Hawk.
59. The Fort Dearborn massacre occurred on August 15, 1812.

night before they marched, they destroyed it. I think it was thrown into the well! If they had fulfilled their word to the Indians, I think they would have gone safe.

On our arrival, I found that the Indians had several prisoners, I advised them to treat them well. We continued our march, and joined the British army below Detroit; and soon after had a fight! The Americans fought well, and drove us with considerable loss! I was surprised at this, as I had been told that the *Americans could not fight!*[60]

Our next movement was against a fortified place. I was stationed, with my braves, to prevent any person going to, or coming from the fort. I found two men taking care of cattle, and took them prisoners. I would not kill them, but delivered them to the British war chief. Soon after, several boats came down the river, full of American soldiers. They landed on the opposite side, took the British batteries, and pursued the soldiers that had left them. They went too far, without knowing the forces of the British, and were *defeated!* I hurried across the river, anxious for an opportunity to show the courage of my braves; but before we reached the ground, all was over! The British had taken many prisoners, *and the Indians were killing them!* I immediately put a stop to it, as I never thought it brave, but cowardly, to kill an unarmed and helpless enemy!

We remained here some time. I cannot detail what took place, as I was stationed, with my braves, in the woods. It appeared, however, that the British could not take this fort—for we were marched to another some distance off. When we approached it, I found it a small *stockade*, and concluded that there were not many men in it. The

60. The Battle of Frenchtown on the Raisin River was on January 22, 1813. In this battle, the Americans suffered more than 400 killed, compared to fewer than forty Indian casualties.

British war chief sent a flag—Colonel Dixon carried it, and returned. He said a young war chief commanded, and would not give up *without fighting!* Dixon came to me and said, "you will see, to-morrow, how easily we will take that fort!" I was of opinion that they would take it; but when the morning came, I was *disappointed.* The British advanced—commenced an attack, and fought like braves; but by braves in the fort, were *defeated,* and a great number killed! The British army were making preparations to retreat. I was now tired of being with them—our success being bad, and having got no plunder.[61] I determined on leaving them and returning to Rock river, to see what had become of my wife and children, as I had not heard from them since I started. That night, I took about twenty of my braves, and left the British camp for home. We met no person on our journey until we reached the Illinois river. Here we found two lodges of Potawatomi. They received us very friendly, and gave us something to eat; and inquired about their friends that were with the British. They said there had been some fighting on the Illinois, and that my old friend, the trader at Peoria, had been taken prisoner! "By Gomo and his party?" I immediately inquired. They said "no; but by the *Americans,* who came up with two boats. They took him and the French settlers, and then burnt the village of Peoria."[62] They could give us no news respecting our people on Rock river. In three days more, we were in the vicinity of our village, when I discovered a smoke ascending from a hollow in the bluffs. I directed my party to proceed to the village, as I wished to

61. American Maj. George Croghan and his soldiers defended Fort Stephenson at Lower Sandusky, Ohio, against the British and Indian warriors on August 2, 1813.

62. Illinois Territorial militia burned down the village of Peoria in October 1812 in what some call the Peoria War.

go alone to the place from whence the smoke proceeded, to see who was there. I approached the spot, and when I came in view of the fire, saw a mat stretched, and an old man sitting under it in sorrow. At any other time, I would have turned away without disturbing him—knowing that he had come there to be *alone*, to humble himself before the Great Spirit, that He might take pity on him! I approached and seated myself beside him. He gave one look at me, and then fixed his eyes on the ground! *It was my old friend!* I anxiously inquired for his son (my adopted child,) and what had befallen our people?[63] My old comrade seemed scarcely alive—he must have fasted a long time. I lighted my pipe, and put it in his mouth. He eagerly drew a few puffs—cast up his eyes, which met mine, and recognized me. His eyes were glassy! He would again have fallen off into forgetfulness, had I not given him some water, which revived him. I again inquired, "what has befallen our people, and what has become of our son?"

In a feeble voice, he said: "Soon after your departure to join the British, I descended the river with a small party, to winter at the place I told you the white man had requested me to come to. When we arrived, I found a fort built, and the white family that had invited me to come and hunt near them, had removed to it. I then paid a visit to the fort, to tell the white people that myself and little band were friendly, and that we wished to hunt in the vicinity of their fort. The war chief who commanded it, told me, that we might hunt on the Illinois side of the Mississippi, and no person would trouble us. That the horsemen only ranged on the Missouri side, and he had

63. The names of Black Hawk's old friend and the adopted son are unknown.

directed them not to cross the river. I was pleased with this assurance of safety, and immediately crossed over and made my winter's camp. Game was plenty; we lived happy, and often talked of you. My boy regretted your absence, and the hardships you would have to undergo. We had been here about two moons, when my boy went out, as usual, to hunt. Night came on, and he did not return! I was alarmed for his safety, and passed a sleepless night. In the morning, my old woman went to the other lodges and gave the alarm—and all turned out in pursuit. There being snow on the ground, they soon came upon his track, and after pursuing it some distance, found he was on the trail of a deer, that led towards the river. They soon came to the place where he had stood and fired, and found a deer hanging upon the branch of a tree, which had been skinned. But here were found the *tracks of white men!* They had taken my boy prisoner. Their tracks led across the river, and then down towards the fort. My friends followed them, and soon found my boy lying dead! He had been most cruelly murdered! His face was shot to pieces—his body stabbed in several places—and his head scalped! His arms were tied behind him!"

The old man paused for some time, and then told me that his wife had died on her way up the Mississippi! I took the hand of my old friend in mine, and pledged myself to avenge the death of his son! It was now dark—a terrible storm commenced raging, with heavy torrents of rain, thunder and lightning. I had taken my blanket off and wrapped it around the old man. When the storm abated, I kindled a fire, and took hold of my old friend to remove him near to it—but *he was dead!* I remained with him the balance of the night. Some of my party came early in the morning to look for me, and assisted me in burying him on the peak of the bluff. I then returned to the village with my friends. I visited the grave of my old friend the last time, as I ascended Rock river.

On my arrival at the village, I was met by the chiefs and braves, and conducted to a lodge that had been prepared to receive me. After eating, I gave an account of what I had seen and done. I explained to them the manner the British and Americans fought. Instead of stealing upon each other, and taking every advantage to *kill the enemy* and *save their own people*, as we do, (which, with us, is considered good policy in a war chief,) they marched out, in open daylight, and *fight*, regardless of the number of warriors they may lose! After the battle is over, they retire to feast, and drink wine, as if nothing had happened; after which, they make a *statement in writing*, of what they have done—each *party claiming the victory!* and neither giving an account of half the number that have been killed on their own side. They all fought like braves, but would not do to *lead a war party* with us. Our maxim is, "to *kill the enemy* and *save our own* men." Those chiefs would do to *paddle* a canoe but not to *steer* it. The Americans shoot better than the British, but their *soldiers* are not so well clothed, or provided for.

The village chief informed me that after I started with my braves and the parties who followed, the nation was reduced to so small a party of fighting men, that they would have been unable to defend themselves, if the Americans had attacked them; that all the women and children, and old men, belonging to the warriors who had joined the British, were left with them to provide for; and that a council was held, which agreed that Quàsh-quà-me, the Lance, and other chiefs, with the old men, women, and children, and such others as chose to accompany them, should descend the Mississippi and go to St. Louis, and place themselves under the protection of the American chief stationed there. They accordingly went down to St. Louis, and were received as the friendly band of our nation—sent up the Missouri, and provided for, whilst their friends were assisting the British!

Ke-o-kuck was then introduced to me as the war-chief of the braves then in the village.[64] I inquired how he had become a chief. They said that a large armed force was seen by their spies, going towards Peoria; that fears were entertained that they would come upon and attack our village; and that a council had been convened to decide upon the best course to be adopted, which concluded upon leaving the village and going on the west side of the Mississippi, to get out of the way. Ke-o-kuck, during the sitting of the council, had been standing at the door of the lodge, (not being allowed to enter, having never killed an enemy,) where he remained until old Wà-co-me came out. He then told him that he had heard what they had decided upon, and was anxious to be permitted to go in and speak, before the council adjourned! Wà-co-me returned, and asked leave for Ke-o-kuck to come in and make a speech. His request was granted. Ke-o-kuck entered, and addressed the chiefs. He said, "I have heard with sorrow, that you have determined to leave our village, and cross the Mississippi, merely because you have been told that the Americans were seen coming in this direction! Would you leave our village, desert our homes, and fly, before an enemy approaches? Would you leave all—even the graves of our fathers, to the mercy of an enemy,

64. Keokuck, "He who has been everywhere," was a mixed-blood Sauk leader who had blue-grey eyes from his Sauk and Sauk-French parents and was about thirteen years younger than Black Hawk. It was well known that he undermined Black Hawk's leadership for personal gain. Donald L. Fixico, "The Black Hawk-Keokuk Controversy," in *Indian Leaders, Oklahoma's First Statesmen*, eds. H. Glen Jordan and Thomas M. Holm (Oklahoma Historical Society, 1979), 64–78.

without *trying to defend them?* Give me charge of your warriors; I'll defend the village, and you may sleep in safety!"

The council consented that Ke-o-kuck should be a war-chief. He marshalled his braves—sent out spies—and advanced with a party himself, on the trail leading to Peoria. They returned without seeing an enemy. The Americans did not come by our village. All were well satisfied with the appointment of Ke-o-kuck. He used every precaution that our people should not be surprised. This is the manner in which, and the cause of, his receiving the appointment.

I was satisfied, and then started to visit my wife and children. I found them well, and my boys were growing finely. It is not customary for us to say much about our women, as they generally perform their part cheerfully, and *never interfere with business belonging to the men!* This is the only wife I ever had, or ever will have. She is a good woman, and teaches my boys to be *brave!*[65] Here I would have rested myself, and enjoyed the comforts of my lodge, but I could not: I had promised to avenge the death of my adopted son!

I immediately collected a party of thirty braves, and explained to them my object in making this war party—it being to avenge the death of my adopted son, who had been cruelly and wantonly murdered by the whites. I explained to them the pledge I had made his father, and told them that they were the last words that he had heard spoken! All were willing to go with me, to fulfil my word. We started in canoes, and descended the Mississippi, until we arrived near the place where fort Madison had stood. It had been abandoned by the whites and burnt; nothing

65. Black Hawk's wife was Asshewaqua, "Singing Bird," a Sauk woman. Her English name was Sarah Baker. She and Black Hawk had five children. Jackson, *Black Hawk: An Autobiography,* 73.

remained but the chimneys.[66] We were pleased to see that the white people had retired from our country. We proceeded down the river again. I landed, with one brave, near Capo Gray; the remainder of the party went to the mouth of the Quiver. I hurried across to the trail that led from the mouth of the Quiver to a fort, and soon after heard firing at the mouth of the creek.[67] Myself and [the] brave concealed ourselves on the side of the road. We had not remained here long, before two men riding one horse, came in full speed from the direction of the sound of the firing. When they came sufficiently near, we fired; the horse jumped, and both men fell! We rushed towards them—one rose and ran. I followed him, and was gaining on him, when he ran over a pile of rails that had lately been made, seized a stick, and struck at me. I now had an opportunity to see his face—I knew him! He had been at Quàsh-quà-me's village to learn his people how to plough. We looked upon him as a good man. I did not wish to kill him, and pursued him no further. I returned and met my brave; he said he had killed the other man, and had his *scalp* in his hand! We had not proceeded far, before we met the man, supposed to be killed, coming up the road, staggering like a drunken man, all covered with blood! This was the most terrible sight I had ever seen. I told my comrade to *kill him,* to put him out of his misery! I could not look at him. I passed on, and heard a rustling in the bushes, and distinctly saw two little boys concealing themselves! I thought of my own children, and passed on without noticing them! My comrade here joined me, and in a little while we met the balance of our party. I told them that we would be pursued,

66. In the late fall of 1813, US soldiers abandoned Fort Madison and burned it as they left.
67. Fort Howard was built at the mouth of the Cuivre River, Missouri.

and directed them to follow me. We crossed the creek, and formed ourselves in the timber. We had not been here long, before a party of mounted men rushed at full speed upon us! I took deliberate aim, and shot the man leading the party. He fell from his horse lifeless! All my people fired, but without effect. The enemy rushed upon us without giving us time to reload. They surrounded us, and forced us to run into a deep sink-hole, at the bottom of which there were some bushes. We loaded our guns, and awaited the approach of the enemy. They rushed to the edge of the hole and fired, killing one of our men. We returned the fire instantly, and killed one of their party! We reloaded, and commenced digging holes in the side of the bank to protect ourselves, whilst a party watched the movements of the enemy, expecting that their whole force would be upon us immediately. Some of my warriors commenced singing their *death-songs!* I heard the whites talking—and called to them, "to come out and fight!" I did not like my situation, and wished the matter settled. I soon heard chopping and knocking. I could not imagine what they were doing. Soon after they run up wheels with a battery on it, and fired down without hurting any of us. I called to them again, and told them if they were "*brave* men, to come down and fight us." They gave up the siege, and returned to their fort about dusk. There were eighteen in this trap with me. We all got out safe, and found one white man dead on the edge of the sink-hole. They did not remove him, for fear of fire. We *scalped* him, and placed our dead man upon him! We could not have left him in a better situation, than on an enemy![68]

68. On May 24, 1815, the Battle of Sink Hole occurred; it was Capt. Peter Craig who was scalped. Jackson, *Black Hawk: An Autobiography*, 75.

We had now effected our purpose, and started back by land—thinking it unsafe to return in our canoes. I found my wife and children, and the greater part of our people, at the mouth of the Ioway river. I now determined to remain with my family, and hunt for them; and humble myself before the Great Spirit, and return thanks to him for preserving me through the war!

I made my hunting camp on English river, (a branch of the Ioway.) During the winter a party of Potawatomi came from the Illinois to pay me a visit—among them was Wàsh-e-own, an old man, that had formerly lived in our village. He informed us, that, in the fall, the Americans had built a fort at Peoria, and had prevented them from going down to the Sangomo to hunt. He said they were very much distressed—that Gomo had returned from the British army, and brought news of their defeat near Malden; and told us that *he* went to the American chief with a flag; gave up fighting, and told the chief that he wished to make peace for his nation. The American chief gave him a paper for the war chief at the fort at Peoria, and I visited that fort with Gomo. It was then agreed that there should be no more fighting between the Americans and Potawatomi; and that two of their chiefs, and eight braves, with five Americans, had gone down to St. Louis to have the peace confirmed. This, said Wàsh-e-own, is good news; for we can now go to our hunting-grounds: and, for my part, I never had anything to do with this war. The Americans never killed any of our people before the war, nor interfered with our hunting grounds; and I resolved to do nothing against them! I made no reply to these remarks, as the speaker was old, and talked like a child!

We gave the Potawatomi a feast. I presented Wàsh-e-own with a good horse; my braves gave one to each of his party, and, at parting, they said they wished us to make peace—

which we did not promise—but told them that we would not send out war parties against the settlements.

A short time after the Potawatomi left, a party of thirty braves, belonging to our nation, from the *peace camp* on the Missouri, paid us a visit. They exhibited *five scalps,* which they had taken on the Missouri, and wished us to dance over them, which we willingly joined in. They related the manner in which they had taken these scalps. Myself and braves then showed the two we had taken, near the Quiver, and told them the reason that induced that war party to go out; as well as the manner, and difficulty we had in obtaining these scalps.

They recounted to us all that had taken place—the number that had been killed by the *peace party,* as they were called and recognized—which far surpassed what our warriors, who had joined the British, had done! This party came for the purpose of joining the British! I advised them to return to the peace party, and told them the news that the Potawatomi had brought. They returned to the Missouri, accompanied by some of my braves, whose families were with the peace party.

After sugar-making was over, in the spring, I visited the Fox village, at the lead mines. They had nothing to do with the war, and were not in mourning. I remained there some days, and spent my time pleasantly with them, in dancing and feasting. I then paid a visit to the Potawatomi village, on the Illinois river, and learned that Sà-na-tu-wa and Tà-ta-puc-key had been to St. Louis. Gomo told me "that peace had been made between his people and the Americans, and that seven of his party remained with the war chief to make the peace stronger!" He then told me that "Wàsh-e-own was dead! That he had been to the fort, to carry some wild fowl, to exchange for tobacco, pipes, etc. That he had got some tobacco and a little flour, and left the fort before sundown; but had not proceeded far before he was *shot dead,* by a war chief who had concealed himself near the path, for that purpose!—and then dragged him to the lake and threw him in, where I afterwards found him. I have since given two horses and my rifle to his relations, not to break the peace—which they had agreed to."

I remained some time at the village with Gomo, and went with him to the fort to pay a visit to the war chief. I spoke the Potawatomi tongue well, and was taken for one of their people by the chief. He treated us very friendly, and said he was very much displeased about the murder of Wàsh-e-own, and would find out, and punish the person that killed him. He made some inquiries about the Sacs, which I answered.

On my return to Rock river, I was informed that a party of soldiers had gone up the Mississippi to build a fort at Prairie du Chien. They had stopped near our village, and appeared to be friendly, and were kindly treated by our people.

We commenced repairing our lodges, putting our village in order, and clearing our cornfields. We divided the fields of the party on the Missouri, among those that wanted, on condition that they should be relinquished to the owners, when they returned from the *peace establishment.* We were again happy in our village: our women went cheerfully to work, and all moved on harmoniously.

Some time afterwards, five or six boats arrived, loaded with soldiers, going to Prairie du Chien, to reinforce the garrison.[69] They appeared friendly, and were well re-

69. The boats that were going upriver to Prairie de Chien on July 21, 1814, were led by Lt. John Campbell. Jackson, *Black Hawk: An Autobiography,* 79.

ceived. We held a council with the war chief. We had no intention of hurting him, or any of his party, or we could easily have defeated them. They remained with us all day, and used, and gave us, plenty of whiskey! During the night a party arrived, (who came down Rock river,) and brought us six kegs of powder! They told us that the British had gone to Prairie du Chien, and taken the fort, and wished us to join them again in the war, which we agreed to. I collected my warriors, and determined to pursue the boats, which had sailed with a fair wind. If we had known the day before, we could easily have them all, as the war chief used no precautions to prevent it. I immediately started with my party, by land, in pursuit—thinking that some of their boats might get aground, or that the Great Spirit would put them in our power, if he wished them taken, and their people killed! About half way up the rapids, I had a full view of the boats, all sailing with a strong wind. I soon discovered that one boat was badly managed, and was suffered to be driven ashore by the wind. They landed, by running hard aground, and lowered their sail. The others passed on. This boat the Great Spirit gave us! We approached it cautiously, and fired upon the men on shore. All that could, hurried aboard, but they were unable to push off, being fast aground. We advanced to the river's bank, under cover, and commenced firing at the boat. Our balls passed through the plank and did execution, as I could hear them screaming in the boat! I encouraged my braves to continue firing. Several guns were fired from the boat, without effect. I prepared my bow and arrows to *throw fire to the sail,* which was lying on the boat; and, after two or three attempts, succeeded in setting the sail on fire.

The boat was soon in flames! About this time, one of the boats that had passed, returned, dropped anchor, and swung in close to the boat on fire, and took off all the people, except those killed and badly wounded. We could distinctly see them passing from one boat to the other, and fired on them with good aim. *We wounded the war chief in this way!* Another boat now came down, dropped her anchor, which did not take hold, and was drifted ashore! The other boat cut her cable and rowed down the river, leaving their comrades without attempting to assist them. We then commenced an attack upon this boat, and fired several rounds. They did not return the fire. We thought they were afraid, or had but a small number on board. I therefore ordered a rush to the boat. When we got near, they *fired,* and killed two of our people, being all that we lost in the engagement. Some of their men jumped out and pushed off the boat, and thus got away without losing a man! I had a good opinion of this war chief—he managed so much better than the others. It would give me pleasure to shake him by the hand.

We now put out the fire on the captured boat, to save the cargo; when a skiff was discovered coming down the river. Some of our people cried out, "here comes an express from Prairie du Chien!" We hoisted the *British flag,* but they would not land. They turned their little boat around, and rowed up the river. We directed a few shots at them, in order to bring them *to;* but they were so far off that we could not hurt them. I found several barrels of whiskey on the captured boat, and knocked in their heads and emptied out the *bad medicine!* I next found a box full of small bottles and packages, which appeared to be *bad medicine* also; such as the *medicine-men* kill the white people with when they get sick. This I threw into the river; and continuing my search for plunder, found several guns, large barrels full of clothing, and some cloth lodges, all of which I distributed among my warriors. We now disposed of the dead, and returned to the Fox village, opposite the lower end of Rock Island; where we put up our new lodges and hoisted the British flag. A great many of our braves were dressed in the uniform clothing which we had taken, which gave our encampment the appearance of a regular camp of soldiers! We placed out sentinels, and commenced dancing over the scalps we had taken. Soon after, several boats passed down; among them, a large boat carrying *big guns!* Our young men followed them some distance, firing at them, but could not do much damage, more than to frighten them. We were now certain that the fort at Prairie du Chien had been taken, as this large boat went up with the first party, who built the fort.[70]

In the course of the day some of the British came down in a small boat; they had followed the large one, thinking she would get fast in the rapids, in which case they were certain of taking her. They had summoned her on the way down to surrender, but she refused; and now, that she had passed over the rapids in safety, all hope of taking her had vanished.

The British landed a *big gun,* and gave us three soldiers to manage it. They complimented us for our bravery in taking the boat, and told us what they had done at Prairie du Chien; gave us a keg of rum, and joined with us in our dancing and feasting! We gave them some things which we had taken from the boat—particularly books and papers. They started the next morning, after promising to return in a few days with a large body of soldiers.

70. During July 17–20, 1814, 150 British soldiers, with about 400 Indian allies, defeated 60 American soldiers at the Battle of Prairie du Chien in Wisconsin. Jackson, *Black Hawk: An Autobiography,* 79.

We went to work, under the directions of the men left with us, and dug up the ground in two places, to put the *big gun* in, that the men might remain in with it, and be safe. We then sent *spies* down the river to reconnoiter, who sent word by a runner, that several boats were coming up, filled with men. I marshalled my forces, and was soon ready for their arrival, and resolved to fight—as we had not yet had a fair fight with the Americans during the war. The boats arrived in the evening, and stopped at a small willow island, nearly opposite to us. During the night we removed our *big gun* further down, and at daylight next morning, commenced firing. We were pleased to see that almost every fire took effect, striking the boats nearly every shot. They pushed off as quick as possible; and I expected would land and give a fight. I was prepared to meet them—but was soon *sadly disappointed!*—the boats having all started down the river. A party of braves followed to watch where they landed; but they did not stop until they got below the Des Moines rapids, when they landed, and commenced building a fort.[71]

I collected a few braves, and started to the place where it was reported they were making a fort. I did not want a fort in our country, as we wished to go down in the fall, to the Two-River country, to hunt—it being our best hunting ground; and we concluded, that if this fort was established, we should be prevented from going to our hunting ground. I arrived in the vicinity of the fort in the evening, and stopped for the night, on the peak of a high bluff. We made no fire, for fear of being observed. Our young men kept watch by turns, whilst the others slept. I was very

71. Cmdr. Zachary Taylor (future 12th President of the United States) built Fort Johnson in the fall of 1814 to control the Sac and Fox Tribes, but it was abandoned a few weeks later. Jackson, *Black Hawk: An Autobiography*, 81.

tired, and soon went to sleep. The Great Spirit, during my slumber, told me to go down the bluff to a creek—that I would there find a hollow tree cut down; to look into the top of it, and I would see a large *snake*—to observe the direction he was looking, and I would see the enemy close by, and unarmed. In the morning, I communicated to my braves what the Great Spirit had told me; and took one of them and went down a hollow that led to the creek, and soon came in sight of the place, on an opposite hill, where they were building the fort. I saw a great many men. We crawled cautiously on our hands and knees, until we got into the bottom—then, through the grass and weeds, until we reached the bank of the creek. Here I found a tree that had been cut down. I looked in the top of it, and saw a large snake, with his head raised, looking across the creek. I raised myself cautiously, and discovered, nearly opposite to me, two war chiefs walking arm-in-arm, without guns. They turned, and walked back towards the place where the men were working at the fort. In a little while they returned, walking immediately towards the spot where we lay concealed—but did not come as near as before. If they had, they would have been killed—for each of us had a good rifle. We crossed the creek, and crawled to a bunch of bushes. I again raised myself a little, to see if they were coming; but they went into the fort. By this they saved their lives.

We recrossed the creek; and I returned alone—going up the hollow we came down. My brave went down the creek; and, on rising a hill to the left of the one we came down, I could plainly see the men at work; and discovered, in the bottom, near the mouth of the creek, a sentinel walking. I watched him attentively, to see if he perceived my companion, who had gone towards him. The sentinel walked first one way and then back again. I observed my brave creeping towards him. The sentinel stopped for some time, and looked in the direction where my brave was concealed. He laid still, and did not move the grass; and, as the sentinel turned to walk, my brave fired and he fell! I looked towards the fort, and saw that they were all in confusion—running in every direction—some down a steep bank to a boat. My comrade joined me, and we returned to the rest of our party, and all hurried back to Rock river, where we arrived in safety at our village. I hung up my *medicine bag*, put away my rifle and spear, and felt as if I should not want them again, as I had no wish to raise any more war parties against the whites, without they gave new provocation. Nothing particular happened from this time until spring, except news that the fort below the rapids had been abandoned and burnt by the Americans.[72]

Soon after I returned from my wintering ground, we received information that *peace* had been made between the British and Americans, and that *we* were required to make peace also—and were invited to go down to Portage des Sioux, for that purpose.[73] Some advised that we should go down—others that we should not. No-mite, our principal civil chief, said he would go, as soon as the Foxes came down from the Mines. They came, and we all started from Rock river. We had not gone far, before our chief was taken sick. We stopped with him at the village on Henderson river. The Foxes went on, and we were to follow as soon as our chief got better; but he continued to get worse, and died. His brother now became the principal chief. He refused to go down—saying, that if he started, he would be taken sick and die, as his brother had done—

72. Fort Madison in the fall of 1813; see page 48 above.
73. The Treaty of Ghent on December 24, 1815, officially ended the War of 1812 between the British and Americans.

which was reasonable! We all concluded, that none of us would go at this time.

The Foxes returned. They said they had smoked the *pipe of peace* with the Americans, and expected that a war party would be sent against us, because we did not go down. This I did not believe; as the Americans had always *lost* by their war parties that came against us.

La Gutrie, and other British traders, arrived at our village on Rock river, in the fall. La Gutrie told us, that we must go down and make peace—that it was the wish of our English father. He said he wished us to go down to the Two-River country to winter—where game was plenty, as there had been no hunting there for several years.

Having heard that a principal war chief, with troops, had come up, and commenced building a fort near Rapids des Moines, we consented to go down with the traders, to see the American chief, and tell him the reason why we had not been down sooner. We arrived at the head of the rapids. Here the traders left their goods and boats, except one, in which they accompanied us to the Americans. We visited the war chief, (he was on board of a boat,) and told him what we had to say—explaining the reason we had not been down sooner. He appeared angry, and talked to La Gutrie for some time. I inquired of him, what the war chief said? He told me that he was threatening to hang him up on the yard-arm of his boat. "But," said he, "I am not afraid of what he says. He dare not put his threats into execution. I have done no more than I had a right to do, as a British subject."

I then addressed the chief, asking permission for ourselves and some Menominee, to go down to the Two-River country to hunt.[74] He said, *we* might go down but must re-

74. Menominee are an Algonquin tribe whose traditional homeland was upper Wisconsin and Michigan. Their population was estimated at 3,000 in the seventeenth century.

turn before the ice made, as he did not intend that we should winter below the fort. "But," said he, "what do you want the Menominee to go with you for?" I did not know, at first, what reply to make—but told him that they had a great many *pretty squaws* with them, and we wished them to go with us on that account! He consented. We all started down the river, and remained *all winter,* as we had no intention of returning before spring, when we asked leave to go. We made a good hunt. Having loaded our traders' boats with furs and peltries, they started to Mackinac, and we returned to our village.

There is one circumstance which I omitted to mention in its proper place. It does not relate to myself or people, but to my friend Gomo, the Potawatomi chief. He came to Rock river to pay me a visit. During his stay, he related to me the following story:

"The war chief at Peoria is a very good man; he always speaks the truth, and treats our people well.[75] He sent for me one day, and told me that he was nearly out of provision, and wished me to send my young men out to hunt, to supply his fort. I promised to do so; and immediately returned to my camp, and told my young men the wishes and wants of the war chief. They readily agreed to go and hunt for our friend; and soon returned with about twenty deer. They carried them to the fort, laid them down at the gate, and returned to our camp. A few days afterwards, I went again to the fort to see if they wanted more meat. The chief gave me some powder and lead, and said he wished me to send my hunters out again. When I returned to my camp, and told my young men that the chief wanted more meat, Má-ta-táh, one of my principal braves,

75. Brig. Gen. Benjamin Howard was the commander at Fort Clark, at Peoria, Illinois, in 1813.

said he would take a party and go across the Illinois [river], about one day's travel, where game was plenty, and make a good hunt for our friend, the war chief. He took eight hunters with him; his wife and several other squaws accompanied them. They had travelled about half the day in the prairie, when they discovered a party of white men coming towards them with a drove of cattle. Our hunters apprehended no danger, or they would have kept out of the way of the whites, (who had not yet perceived them.) Má-ta-táh changed his course, as he wished to meet and speak to the whites. As soon as the whites saw our party, some of them put off at full speed, and came up to our hunters. Má-ta-táh gave up his gun to them, and endeavored to explain to them that he was friendly, and was hunting for the war chief. They were not satisfied with this, but fired at and wounded him. He got into the branch of a tree that had been blown down, to keep the horses from running over him. He was again fired on by several guns and badly wounded. He found that he would be murdered, (if not mortally wounded already,) and sprung at the nearest man to him, seized his gun, and shot him from his horse. He then fell, covered with blood from his wounds, and almost instantly expired!

"The other hunters, being in the rear of Má-ta-táh, seeing that the whites had killed him, endeavored to make their escape. They were pursued, and nearly all the party *murdered!* My youngest brother brought in the news in the night, he having been with the hunters, and got but slightly wounded. He said the whites had abandoned their cattle, and gone back towards the settlement. The remainder of the night was spent in lamenting for the deaths of our friends. At daylight, I blacked my face, and started to the fort to see the war chief. I met him at the gate, and told him what had happened. His countenance changed;

I could see sorrow depicted in it for the death of my people. He tried to persuade me that I was mistaken, as he 'could not believe that the whites would act so cruelly.' But when I convinced him, he told me that those '*cowards* who had murdered my people should be punished.' I told him that my people would have *revenge—that* they would not trouble any of his people of the fort, as we did not blame him or any of his soldiers—but that a party of my braves would go towards the Wabash to avenge the death of their friends and relations. The next day I took a party of hunters and killed several deer, and left them at the fort gate as I passed."

Here Gomo ended his story. I could relate many similar ones that have come within my own knowledge and observation; but I dislike to look back and bring on sorrow afresh. I will resume my narrative.

The great chief at St. Louis having sent word for us to go down and confirm the treaty of peace, we did not hesitate, but started immediately, that we might smoke the *peace-pipe* with him.[76] On our arrival, we met the great chiefs in council. They explained to us the words of our Great Father in Washington, accusing us of heinous crimes and diverse misdemeanors, particularly in not coming

76. William Clark was in command at St. Louis. *Black Hawk: An Autobiography*, 102. After Clark's return with Meriwether Lewis from their expedition exploring the Missouri River, Clark was placed in command at St. Louis in 1807 as well as being appointed Indian agent, and he served in both capacities until the 1820s. In 1813, President James Madison appointed Clark as the Governor of the newly formed Missouri Territory and President James Monroe reappointed Clark as Governor in 1820, although Missouri became the twenty-fourth state the following year. In 1822, President Monroe appointed Clark as the Superintendent of Indian Affairs due to his familiarity with American Indian tribes. Jerome Steffen, *William Clark: Jeffersonian Man on the Frontier* (University of Oklahoma Press, 1977), 89-95.

down when first invited. We knew very well that *our Great Father had deceived us,* and thereby *forced* us to join the British, and could not believe that he had put this speech into the mouths of these chiefs to deliver to us. I was not a civil chief, and consequently made no reply: but our chiefs told the commissioners that "what they had said was a lie!—that our Great Father had sent no such speech, he knowing the situation in which we had been placed had been *caused by him!*" The white chiefs appeared very angry at this reply, and said they "would break off the treaty with us, and go *to war,* as they would not be insulted."

Our chiefs had no intention of insulting them, and told them—"that they merely wished to explain to them that *they had told a lie,* without making them angry; in the same manner that the whites do, when they do not believe what is told them!" The council then proceeded, and the pipe of peace was smoked.

Here, for the first time, I touched the goose quill to the treaty—not knowing, however, that, by that act, I consented to give away my village. Had that been explained to me, I should have opposed it, and never would have signed their treaty, as my recent conduct will clearly prove.[77]

What do we know of the manner of the laws and customs of the white people? They might buy our bodies for dissection, and we would touch the goose quill to confirm

77. The agreement that Black Hawk signed was the Treaty of 1816. Charles Kappler, ed., "Treaty with the Sauk, 1816, May 13, 1816," in *Indian Treaties 1778–1883* (Interland Publishing Inc., 1972), 126–28. Unbeknownst to Black Hawk, Clark took the opportunity to insert language affirming the land cession provisions of the Treaty of 1804 into the new treaty. J. Gerald Kennedy, ed., *Life of Black Hawk* (Penguin Books, 2008), 104, note 54.

it, without knowing what we are doing. This was the case with myself and people in touching the goose quill the first time.

We can only judge of what is proper and right by our standard of right and wrong, which differs widely from the whites, if I have been correctly informed. The whites *may do bad* all their lives, and then, if they are *sorry for it* when about to die, *all is well!* But with us it is different: we must continue throughout our lives to do what we conceive to be good. If we have corn and meat, and know of a family that have none, we divide with them. If we have more blankets than sufficient, and others have not enough, we must give to them that want. But I will presently explain our customs and the manner we live.

We were friendly treated by the white chiefs, and started back to our village on Rock river. Here we found that troops had arrived to build a fort at Rock Island.[78] This, in our opinion, was a contradiction to what we had done—"to prepare for war in time of peace." We did not, however, object to their building the fort on the island, but we were very sorry, as this was the best island on the Mississippi, and had long been the resort of our young people during the summer. It was our garden (like the white people have near to their big villages) which supplied us with strawberries, blackberries, gooseberries, plums, apples, and nuts of different kinds; and its waters supplied us with fine fish, being situated in the rapids of the river. In my early life, I spent many happy days on this island. A good spirit had care of it, who lived in a cave in the rocks immediately under the place where the fort now stands, and has often been seen by our people. He was

78. Fort Armstrong was constructed on Rock Island in 1816. Jackson, *Black Hawk: An Autobiography*, 87.

white, with large wings like a *swan's*, but ten times larger. We were particular not to make much noise in that part of the island which he inhabited, for fear of disturbing him. But the noise of the fort has since driven him away, and no doubt a *bad spirit* has taken his place!

Our village was situated on the north side of Rock river, at the foot of its rapids, and on the point of land between Rock river and the Mississippi. In its front, a prairie extended to the bank of the Mississippi; and in our rear, a continued bluff, gently ascending from the prairie. On its highest peak our Watch Tower was situated, from which we had a fine view for many miles up and down Rock river, and every direction.[79] On the side of this bluff we had our corn-fields, extending about two miles up, running parallel with the Mississippi; where we joined those of the Foxes, whose village was on the bank of the Mississippi, opposite the lower end of Rock island, and three miles distant from ours. We had about eight hundred acres in cultivation, including what we had on the islands of Rock river. The land around our village, uncultivated, was covered with bluegrass, which made excellent pasture for our horses. Several fine springs broke out of the bluff, near by, from which we were supplied with good water. The rapids of Rock river furnished us with an abundance of excellent fish, and the land, being good, never failed to produce good crops of corn, beans, pumpkins, and squashes. We always had plenty—our children never cried with hunger, nor our people were never in want. Here our village had stood for more than a hundred years, during all which time we were the undisputed possessors of the valley of the Mississippi, from the Wisconsin to the

79. This sentence was inserted in the 1882 edition of Black Hawk's autobiography.

Portage des Sioux, near the mouth of the Missouri, being about seven hundred miles in length.

At this time we had very little intercourse with the whites, except our traders. Our village was healthy, and there was no place in the country possessing such advantages, nor no hunting grounds better than those we had in possession. If another prophet had come to our village in those days, and told us what has since taken place, none of our people would have believed him! What! to be driven from our village and hunting grounds, and not even permitted to visit the graves of our forefathers, our relations and friends?

This hardship is not known to the whites. With us it is a custom to visit the graves of our friends, and keep them in repair for many years. The mother will go alone to weep over the grave of her child! The brave, with pleasure, visits the grave of his father, after he has been successful in war, and repaints the post that shows where he lies! There is no place like that where the bones of our forefathers lie, to go to when in grief. Here the Great Spirit will take pity on us!

But, how different is our situation now, from what it was in those days! Then we were as happy as the buffalo on the plains—but now, we are as miserable as the hungry, howling wolf in the prairie! But I am digressing from my story. Bitter reflection crowds upon my mind, and must find utterance.

When we returned to our village in the spring, from our wintering grounds, we would finish trading with our traders, who always followed us to our village. We purposely kept some of our fine furs for this trade; and, as there was great opposition among them, who should get these skins, we always got our goods cheap. After this trade was over, the traders would give us a few kegs of rum, which was generally promised in the fall, to encourage us to make a good hunt, and not go to war. They would then start with their furs and peltries for their homes. Our old men would take a frolic, (at this time our young men never drank.) When this was ended, the next thing to be done was to bury our dead, (such as had died during the year.) This is a great *medicine feast.* The relations of those who have died, give all the goods they have purchased, as presents to their friends—thereby reducing themselves to poverty, to show the Great Spirit that they are humble, so that he will take pity on them.[80] We would next open the cashes, and take out corn and other provisions, which had been put up in the fall,—and then commence repairing our lodges. As soon as this is accomplished, we repair the fences around our fields, and clean them off, ready for planting corn. This work is done by our women. The men, during this time, are feasting on dried venison, bear's meat, wild fowl, and corn, prepared in different ways; and recounting to each other what took place during the winter.

Our women plant the corn, and as soon as they get done, we make a feast, and dance the *crane* dance, in which they join us, dressed in their best, and decorated with feathers.[81] At this feast our young braves select the

80. The Medicine Feast was held with the objective that the Great Spirit would bless and protect the Sauk from bad luck and evil. The spirit of a person who died "traveled to the West." An adoption ceremony was held to include another individual to replace the dead relative, who looked like the deceased or had the mannerism of the deceased. The adopted person did not live with the family but was included in all family events as a part of the adoption ceremony.

81. The Crane Dance announces the new season and remains one of the most important ceremonies of the Sac and Fox Nation. It is followed by another ceremony called the National Dance, according to Black Hawk. This dance is for warriors to express their recent exploits in battle and killing an enemy.

young woman they wish to have for a wife. He then informs his mother, who calls on the mother of the girl, when the arrangement is made, and the time appointed for him to come. He goes to the lodge when all are asleep, (or pretend to be,) lights his matches, which have been provided for the purpose, and soon finds where his intended sleeps. He then awakens her, and holds the light to his face that she may know him—after which he places the light close to her. If she blows it out, the ceremony is ended, and he appears in the lodge next morning, as one of the family. If she does not blow out the light, but leaves it to burn out, he retires from the lodge. The next day he places himself in full view of it, and plays his flute. The young women go out, one by one, to see who he is playing for. The tune changes, to let them know that he is not playing for them. When his intended makes her appearance at the door, he continues his *courting* tune, until she returns to the lodge. He then gives over playing, and makes another trial at night, which generally turns out favorable. During the first year they ascertain whether they can agree with each other, and can be happy—if not, they part, and each looks out again. If we were to live together and disagree, we should be as foolish as the whites! No indiscretion can banish a woman from her parental lodge—no difference how many children she may bring home, she is always welcome—the kettle is over the fire to feed them.

The crane dance often lasts two or three days. When this is over, we feast again, and have our *national* dance. The large square in the village is swept and prepared for the purpose. The chiefs and old warriors, take seats on mats which have been spread at the upper end of the square—the drummers and singers come next, and the braves and women form the sides, leaving a large space in the middle. The drums beat, and the singers commence. A warrior enters the square, keeping time with the music. He shows the manner he started on a war party—how he approached the enemy—he strikes, and describes the way he killed him. All join in applause. He then leaves the square, and another enters and takes his place. Such of our young men as have not been out in war parties, and killed an enemy, stand back ashamed—not being able to enter the square. I remember that I was ashamed to look where our young women stood, before I could take my stand in the square as a warrior.

What pleasure it is to an old warrior, to see his son come forward and relate his exploits—it makes him feel young, and induces him to enter the square, and "fight his battles o'er again."

This national dance makes our warriors. When I was travelling last summer, on a steam boat, on a large river, going from New York to Albany, I was shown the place where the Americans dance their national dance [West Point]; where the old warriors recount to their young men, what they have done, to stimulate them to go and do likewise. This surprised me, as I did not think the whites understood our way of making braves.

When our national dance is over—our corn-fields hoed, and every weed dug up, and our corn about knee-high, all our young men would start in a direction towards sun-down, to hunt deer and buffalo—being prepared, also, to kill Sioux if any are found on our hunting grounds—a part of our old men and women to the lead mines to make lead—and the remainder of our people start to fish, and get mat stuff.[82] Every one leaves the village, and re-

82. "mat stuff": reeds. The Sioux were one of the larger American Indian groups with an estimated population of more than 20,000 in 1800. They spanned the Great Lakes region, upper Midwest, and into the northern Plains. They were a traditional enemy of the Sauk and Fox.

mains about forty days. They then return: the hunting party bringing in dried buffalo and deer meat, and sometimes *Sioux scalps,* when they are found trespassing on our hunting grounds. At other times they are met by a party of Sioux too strong for them, and are driven in. If the Sioux have killed the Sacs last, they expect to be retaliated upon, and will fly before them, and vice versa. Each party knows that the other has a right to retaliate, which induces those who have killed last,. to give way before their enemy—as neither wish to strike, except to avenge the death of their relatives. All our wars are predicated by the relatives of those killed; or by aggressions upon our hunting grounds.

The party from the lead mines bring lead, and the others dried fish, and mats for our winter lodges. Presents are now made by each party; the first, giving to the others dried buffalo and deer, and they, in exchange, presenting them with lead, dried fish and mats. This is a happy season of the year—having plenty of provisions, such as beans, squashes, and other produce, with our dried meat and fish, we continue to make feasts and visit each other, until our corn is ripe. Some lodge in the village makes a feast daily, to the Great Spirit. I cannot explain this so that the white people would comprehend me, as we have no regular standard among us. Every one makes his feast as he thinks best, to please the Great Spirit, who has the care of all beings created. Others believe in two Spirits: one good and one bad, and make feasts for the Bad Spirit, *to keep him quiet!* If they can make peace with him, the Good Spirit will not hurt them! For my part, I am of opinion, that so far as we have *reason,* we have a right to use it, in determining what is right or wrong; and should pursue that path which we believe to be right—believing that, "whatever is, is right." If the Great and Good Spirit wished us to believe and do as the whites, he could easily change our opinions, so that we would see, and think, and act as they do. We are *nothing* compared to His power, and we feel and know it. We have men among us, like the whites, who pretend to know the right path, but will not consent to show it without *pay!* I have no faith in their paths—but believe that every man must make his own path!

When our corn is getting ripe, our young people watch with anxiety for the signal to pull roasting ears—as none dare touch them until the proper time. When the corn is fit to use, another great ceremony takes place, with feasting, and returning thanks to the Great Spirit for giving us corn.[83]

I will here relate the manner in which corn first came. According to tradition, handed down to our people, a beautiful woman was seen to descend from the clouds, and alight upon the earth, by two of our ancestors, who had killed a deer, and were sitting by a fire, roasting a part of it to eat. They were astonished at seeing her, and concluded that she must be hungry, and had smelt the meat—and immediately went to her, taking with them a piece of the roasted venison. They presented it to her, and she eat—and told them to return to the spot where she was sitting, at the end of one year, and they would find a reward for their kindness and generosity. She then ascended to the clouds, and disappeared. The two men returned to their village, and explained to the nation what they had seen, done, and heard—but were laughed at by their people. When the period arrived, for them to visit this consecrated ground, where they were to find a reward

83. The Green Corn Ceremony was and is conducted over four days starting with purification of the people's bodies, dancing to pay homage to the Great Spirit, and feasting to celebrate the gift of the harvest of corn.

for their attention to the beautiful woman of the clouds, they went with a large party, and found, where her right hand had rested on the ground, *corn* growing—and where the left hand had rested, *beans,*—and immediately where she had been seated, *tobacco.*

The two first have, ever since, been cultivated by our people, as our principal provisions—and the last used for smoking. The white people have since found out the latter, and seem to relish it as much as we do—as they use it in different ways, viz. smoking, snuffing and eating!

We thank the Great Spirit for all the benefits he has conferred upon us. For myself, I never take a drink of water from a spring, without being mindful of his goodness.

We next have our great ball play—from three to five hundred on a side, play this game.[84] We play for horses, guns, blankets, or any other kind of property we have. The successful party take the stakes, and all retire to our lodges in peace and friendship.

We next commence horse-racing, and continue our sport and feasting, until the corn is all secured. We then prepare to leave our village for our hunting grounds. The traders arrive, and give us credit for such articles as we want to clothe our families, and enable us to hunt. We first, however, hold a council with them, to ascertain the price they will give us for our skins, and what they will charge us for goods. We inform them where we intend hunting—and tell them where to build their houses. At this place, we deposit part of our corn, and leave our old people. The traders have always been kind to them, and relieved them when in want. They were always much respected by our people—and never since we have been a nation, has one of them been killed by any of our people.

84. Lacrosse.

We disperse, in small parties, to make our hunt, and as soon as it is over, we return to our traders' establishment, with our skins, and remain feasting, playing cards and other pastimes, until near the close of the winter. Our young men then start on the beaver hunt; others to hunt raccoons and muskrats—and the remainder of our people go to the sugar camps to make sugar. All leave our encampment, and appoint a place to meet on the Mississippi, so that we may return to our village together, in the spring. We always spent our time pleasantly at the sugar camp. It being the season for wild fowl, we lived well, and always had plenty, when the hunters came in, that we might make a feast for them. After this is over, we return to our village, accompanied, sometimes, by our traders. In this way, the year rolled round happily. But these are times that were!

On returning, in the spring, from our hunting ground, I had the pleasure of meeting our old friend, the trader of Peoria, at Rock Island. He came up in a boat from St. Louis, not as a trader, as in times past, but as our *agent.* We were all pleased to see him. He told us, that he narrowly escaped falling into the hands of Dixon. He remained with us a short time, gave us good advice, and then returned to St. Louis.

The Sioux having committed depredations on our people, we sent out war parties that summer, who succeeded in killing *fourteen.* I paid several visits to fort Armstrong during the summer, and was always well treated. We were not as happy then in our village as formerly. Our people got more liquor than customary. I used all my influence to prevent drunkenness, but without effect. As the settlements progressed towards us, we became worse off, and more unhappy. Many of our people, instead of going to their old hunting grounds, where game was plenty, would go near to the settlements to hunt—and, instead of saving their skins to pay the trader for goods furnished them in the fall, would sell them to the settlers for whiskey! and return in the spring with their families, almost naked, and without the means of getting any thing for them.

About this time my eldest son was taken sick and died. He had always been a dutiful child, and had just grown to manhood. Soon after, my youngest daughter, an interesting and affectionate child, died also. This was a hard stroke, because I loved my children.[85] In my distress, I left the noise of the village, and built my lodge on a mound in my corn-field, and enclosed it with a fence, around which I planted corn and beans. Here I was with my family alone. I gave every thing I had away, and reduced myself to poverty. The only covering I retained, was a piece of buffalo robe. I resolved on blacking my face and fasting, for two years, for the loss of my two children—drinking only of water in the middle of the day, and eating sparingly of boiled corn at sunset. I fulfilled my promise, hoping that the Great Spirit would take pity on me.

My nation had now some difficulty with the Ioways, with whom we wished to be at peace.[86] Our young men had repeatedly killed some of the Ioways; and these breaches had always been made up by giving presents to the rela-

85. The name of Black Hawk's oldest son was Nameequa, or Whirling Thunder, and the name of his youngest daughter was Nauasia. Black Hawk and his wife, As-she-we-qua, "Singing Bird," had five children: Gamesett, Nameequa, Nauasia, Whirling Thunder, and Nashashuk, also known as Joseph Young Bird. Donald Ricky, *Native Peoples A to Z: A Reference Guide to Native Peoples of the Western Hemisphere, Vol. 1* (North American Book Distributors, LLC, 2019), 312–15.

86. The population of the Ioways was estimated to be only 800 by the early 1800s. Prior to European contact, they moved from their ancestral homelands in southern Wisconsin to Iowa, the state that bears their name.

tions of those killed. But the last council we had with them, we promised that, in case any more of their people were killed by ours, instead of presents, we would give up the person, or persons, that had done the injury. We made thus determination known to our people; but, notwithstanding, one of our young men killed an Ioway the following winter.

A party of our people were about starting for the Ioway village to give the young man up. I agreed to accompany them. When we were ready to start, I called at the lodge for the young man to go with us. He was sick, but willing to go. His brother, however, prevented him, and insisted on going to die in his place, as he was unable to travel. We started, and on the seventh day arrived in sight of the Ioway village, and within a short distance of it, halted and dismounted. We all bid farewell to our young brave, who entered the village alone, singing his *death-song*, and sat down on the square in the middle of the village.[87] One of the Ioway chiefs came out to us. We told him that we had fulfilled our promise—that we had brought the brother of the young man who had killed one of their people—that he had volunteered to come in his place, in consequence of his brother being unable to travel from sickness. We had no further conversation, but mounted our horses and rode off. As we started, I cast my eye toward the village, and observed the Ioway coming out of their lodges with spears and war clubs. We took our trail back, and travelled until dark—then encamped and made a fire. We had not been here long, before we heard the sound of horses coming towards us. We seized our arms;

87. Normally Sauk warriors had a personal death song that they would sing if they sensed that they would soon die, thus preparing their body to enter a spiritual realm while leaving the living world.

but instead of any enemy, it was our young brave with two horses. He told me that after we had left him, they menaced him with death for some time—then gave him something to eat—smoked the pipe with him and made him a present of the two horses and some goods, and started him after us. When we arrived at our village, our people were much pleased; and for the noble and generous conduct of the Ioways, on this occasion, not one of their people has become killed since by any of our nation.

That fall I visited Malden with several of my band, and were well treated by the agent of our British Father, who gave us a variety of presents. He also gave me a medal, and told me there never would be war between England and America again; but, for my fidelity to the British during the war that had terminated some before, requested me to come with my band every year and get presents, as Col. Dixon had promised me.

I returned, and hunted that winter on the Two-Rivers. The whites were now settling the country fast. I was out one day hunting in a bottom, and met three white men. They accused me of killing their hogs. I denied it; but they would not listen to me. One of them took my gun out of my hand and fired it off—then took out the flint, gave back my gun, and commenced beating me with sticks, and ordered me off. I was so much bruised that I could not sleep for several nights.

Some time after this occurrence, one of my camp cut a bee-tree, and carried the honey to his lodge. A party of white men soon followed, and told him the bee-tree was theirs, and that he had no right to cut it. He pointed to the honey and told them to take it; they were not satisfied with this, but took all the packs of skins that he had collected during the winter, to pay his trader and clothe his family with in the spring, and carried them off!

How could we like such people, who treated us so unjustly? We determined to break up our camp, for fear that they would do worse—and when we joined our people in the spring, a great many of them complained of similar treatment.

This summer our agent came to live at Rock Island. He treated us well, and gave us good advice. I visited him and the trader very often during the summer, and, for the first time, heard talk of our having to leave my village. The trader, explained to me the terms of the treaty that had been made, and said we would be obliged to leave the Illinois side of the Mississippi, and advised us to select a good place for our village, and remove to it in the spring.[88] He pointed out the difficulties we would have to encounter if we remained at our village on Rock river. He had great influence with the principal Fox chief, his adopted brother, and persuaded him to leave his village, go to the west side of the Mississippi river and build another—which he did the spring following.

Nothing was now talked of but leaving our village. Ke-o-kuck had been persuaded to consent to go; and was using all his influence, backed by the war chief at fort Armstrong and our agent and trader at Rock Island, to induce others to go with him. He sent the crier through the village to inform our people that it was the wish of our Great Father that we should remove to the west side of the Mississippi—and recommended the Ioway river as a good place for the new village—and wished his party to make such arrangements, before they started on their

88. Kappler, "Treaty With the Sauk and Foxes, 1804," 74–77. Agent Thomas Forsyth arrived in the summer of 1819; the trader was George Davenport, a English settler who founded the Iowa city that bears his name. J. Gerald Kennedy, *Life of Black Hawk*, 104.

winter's hunt, as to preclude the necessity of their returning to the village in the spring.

The party opposed to removing called upon me for my opinion. I gave it freely—and after questioning Quàsh-quà-me about the sale of our lands, he assured me that he "never had consented to the sale of our village." I now promised this party to be their leader, and raised the standard of opposition to Ke-o-kuck, with a full determination not to leave my village. I had an interview with Ke-o-kuck, to see if this difficulty could not be settled with our Great Father—and told him to propose to give other land, (any that our Great Father might choose, even our *lead mines,*) to be peaceably permitted to keep the small point of land on which our village and lands were situate[d]. I was of opinion that the white people had plenty of land, and would never take our village from us. Ke-o-kuck promised to make an exchange if possible; and applied to our agent, and the great chief at St. Louis, (who has charge of all the agents,) for permission to go to Washington to see our Great Father for that purpose. This satisfied us for some time. We started to our hunting grounds, in good hopes that something would be done for us. During the winter I received information that three families of whites had arrived at our village and destroyed some of our lodges, and were making fences and dividing our corn-fields for their own *use—and were quarreling among themselves about their lines in the division!* I immediately started for Rock river, a distance of ten days' travel, and on my arrival found the report to be true. I went to my lodge, and saw a family occupying it. I wished to talk with them, but they could not understand me. I then went to Rock Island, and (the agent being absent,) told the interpreter what I wanted to say to these people, viz: "Not to settle on our lands—nor trouble our lodges or fences—that there was plenty of land in the country for them to settle upon—and they must leave our village, as we were coming back to it in the spring." The interpreter wrote me a paper, and I went back to the village, and showed it to the intruders, but could not understand their reply. I expected, however, that they would remove, as I requested them. I returned to Rock Island, passed the night there, and had a long conversation with the trader. He again advised me to give up, and make my village with Ke-o-kuck, on the Ioway river. I told him that I would not. The next morning I crossed the Mississippi, on very bad ice—but the Great Spirit made it strong, that I might pass over safe. I travelled three days farther to see the Winnebago sub-agent, and converse with him on the subject of our difficulties. He gave me no better news than the trader had done. I started then, by way of Rock river, to see the prophet, believing that he was a man of great knowledge.[89] When we met, I explained to him every thing as it was. He at once agreed that I was right, and advised me never to give up our village, for the whites to plough up the bones of our people. He said, that if we remained at our village, the whites would not trouble us—and advised me to get Ke-o-kuck, and the party that had consented to go with him to the Ioway in the spring, to return, and remain at our village.

89. The prophet was White Cloud, sometimes called the Winnebago prophet, also known as Wabokieshiek. White Cloud's father was a Sauk and his mother was a Winnebago. From this point on, when Black Hawk mentions the prophet, he is referring to White Cloud. The role of White Cloud in Native patriotism has been underestimated. Similar to the Shawnee Prophet who convinced warriors of different tribes to join his brother, Tecumseh, during the War of 1812, Black Hawk in early 1832 believed in White Cloud and his similar prophecy. White Cloud told Black Hawk about his dream that the British and those tribes mistreated by white settlers would join in a campaign for Indians to take back their homelands.

I returned to my hunting ground, after an absence of one moon, and related what I had done. In a short time we came up to our village, and found that the whites had not left it—but that others had come, and that the greater part of our corn-fields had been enclosed. When we landed, the whites appeared displeased because we came back. We repaired the lodges that had been left standing, and built others. Ke-o-kuck came to the village; but his object was to persuade others to follow him to the Ioway. He had accomplished nothing towards making arrangements for us to remain, or to exchange other lands for our village. There was no more friendship existing between us. I looked upon him as a coward, and no brave, to abandon his village to be occupied by strangers. What *right* had these people to our village, and our fields, which the Great Spirit had given us to live upon?

My reason teaches me that *land cannot be sold.* The Great Spirit gave it to his children to live upon, and cultivate as far as is necessary for their subsistence; and so long as they occupy and cultivate it, they have the right to the soil—but if they voluntarily leave it, then any other people have a right to settle upon it. Nothing can be sold but such things as can be carried away.[90]

In consequence of the improvements of the intruders on our fields, we found considerable difficulty to get ground to plant a little corn. Some of the whites permitted us to plant small patches in the fields they had fenced, keeping all the best ground for themselves. Our women had great difficulty in climbing their fences, (being unaccustomed to the kind,) and were ill-treated if they left a rail down.

90. Black Hawk viewed land in a deeper context of the earth rather than a commodity to be bought, sold, or traded. Black Hawk, like many Native people, saw himself as a part of Mother Earth.

One of my old friends thought he was safe. His cornfield was on a small island of Rock river. He planted his corn; it came up well—but the white man saw it!—he wanted the island, and took his team over, ploughed up the corn, and re-planted it for himself! The old man shed tears; not for himself but the distress his family would be in if they raised no corn.[91]

The white people brought whisky into our village, made our people drunk, and cheated them out of their horses, guns, and traps! This fraudulent system was carried to such an extent that I apprehended serious difficulties might take place, unless a stop was put to it. Consequently, I visited all the whites and begged them not to sell whisky to my people. One of them continued the practice openly. I took a party of my young men, went to his house, and took out his barrel and broke in the head and poured out the whisky. I did this for fear some of the whites might be killed by my people when drunk.[92]

Our people were treated badly by the whites on many occasions. At one time, a white man beat one of our women cruelly, for pulling a few suckers of corn out of his field, to suck, when hungry! At another time, one of our young men was beat with clubs by two white men for opening a fence which crossed our road, to take his horse through. His shoulder blade was broken, and his body badly bruised, from which he soon after *died!*

Bad, and cruel, as our people were treated by the whites, not one of them was hurt or molested by any of

91. Corn reached the early Native peoples of the Lower Great Lakes about 800 to 1000 AD. See Michael Blake, *Maize for the Gods: Unearthing the 9,000-Year History of Corn* (University of California Press, 2015).
92. For the impact of alcohol on Native people in early America, see Peter C. Mancall, *Deadly Medicine: Indians and Alcohol in Early America* (Cornell University Press, 1997).

my band. I hope this will prove that we are a peaceable people—having permitted ten men to take possession of our corn-fields; prevent us from planting corn; burn and destroy our lodges; ill-treat our women; and *beat to death* our men, without offering resistance to their barbarous cruelties. This is a lesson worthy for the white man to learn: to use forbearance when injured.

We acquainted our agent daily with our situation, and through him, the great chief at St. Louis—and hoped that something would be done for us.[93] The whites were *complaining* at the same time that *we* were *intruding* upon *their rights!* THEY made themselves out the *injured* party, and *we* the *intruders!* and called loudly to the great war chief to protect *their* property!

How smooth must be the language of the whites, when they can make right look like wrong, and wrong like right.

During this summer, I happened at Rock Island when a great chief arrived, whom I had known as the great chief of Illinois, [governor Cole] in company with another chief, who, I have been told, is a great writer [judge Jas. Hall.][94] I called upon them and begged to explain to them the grievances, under which me and my people were laboring, hoping that they could do something for us. The great chief, however, did not seem disposed to counsel with me. He said he was no longer the great chief of Illinois—that his children had selected another father in his stead, and that he now only ranked as they did. I

93. Agent Thomas Forsyth and William Clark in St. Louis.

94. Governor Edward Coles of Illinois served from 1822 to 1826. James Hall practiced law and edited a newspaper in Illinois. He would write a number of books in the 1830s and 1840s, including *History of the Indian Tribes of North America,* in which he mentions meeting Black Hawk as well as the mistreatment of his tribe by white settlers. J. Gerald Kennedy, *Life of Black Hawk,* 105, note 62.

was surprised at this talk, as I had always heard that he was a good, brave, and great chief. But the white people never appear to be satisfied. When they get a good father, they hold councils, (at the suggestion of some bad, ambitious man, who wants the place himself,) and conclude, among themselves that this man, or some other equally ambitious, would make a better father than they have, and nine times out of ten they don't get as good a one again.

I insisted on explaining to these two chiefs the true situation of my people. They gave their assent: I rose and made a speech, in which I explained to them the treaty made by Quàshquà-me, and three of our braves, according to the manner the trader and others had explained it to me. I then told them that Quàsh-quà-me and his party *denied*, positively, having ever sold my village; and that, as I had never known them to *lie*, I was determined to keep it in possession.

I told them that the white people had already entered our village, *burnt our lodges, destroyed our fences, ploughed up our corn, and beat our people:* that they had brought *whisky* into our country, *made our people drunk*, and taken from them their *horses, guns*, and *traps;* and that I had borne all this injury, without suffering any of my braves to raise a hand against the whites.[95]

My object in holding this council, was to get the opinion of these two chiefs, as to the best course for me to pursue. I had appealed in vain, time after time, to our agent, who regularly represented our situation to the great chief at St. Louis, whose duty it was to call upon our Great Father to have justice done to us; but instead of this, we are told

95. Whiskey was introduced to the Sac and Fox by fur traders in the 1770s or earlier. For trade in general, see William T. Hagan, *The Sac and Fox Indians* (University of Oklahoma Press, 1958), 11-15.

that the white people want our country and we must leave it to them!

I did not think it possible that our Great Father wished us to leave our village, where we had lived so long, and where the bones of so many of our people had been laid. The great chief said that, as he was no longer a chief, he could do nothing for us; and felt sorry that it was not in his power to aid us—nor did he know how to advise us. Neither of them could do any thing for us; but both evidently appeared very sorry. It would give me great pleasure, at all times, to take these two chiefs by the hand.

That fall I paid a visit to the agent, before we started to our hunting grounds, to hear if he had any good news for me. He had news! He said that the land on which our village stood was now ordered to be sold to individuals; and that, when sold, *our right* to remain, by treaty, would be at an end, and that if we returned next spring, we would be *forced* to remove!

We learned during the winter that *part* of the lands where our village stood had become sold to individuals, and that the *trader* at Rock Island had bought the greater part that had been sold.[96] The reason was now plain to me why *he* urged us to remove. His object, we thought, was to get our lands. We held several councils that winter to determine what we should do, and resolved, in one of them, to return to our village in the spring, as usual; and concluded, that if we were removed by force, that the *trader*, agent, and others, must be the cause; and that, if found guilty of having us driven from our village they should be *killed!* The trader stood foremost on this list. He had pur-

96. George Davenport was the trader. Roger L. Nichols, *Black Hawk and the Warrior's Path* (Harlan Davidson, Inc., 1992), 83. See page 77, note 88, above.

chased the land on which my lodge stood, and that of our *grave yard* also! Ne-a-pope promised to kill him, the agent, the interpreter, the great chief at St. Louis, the war chief at fort Armstrong, Rock Island, and Ke-o-kuck—these being the principal persons to blame for endeavoring to remove us.[97]

Our women received bad accounts from the women that had been raising corn at the new village—the difficulty of breaking the new prairie with hoes—and the small quantity of corn raised. We were nearly in the same situation in regard to the latter, it being the first time I ever knew our people to be in want of provision.

I prevailed upon some of Ke-o-kuck's band to return this spring to the Rock river village. Ke-o-kuck would not return with us. I hoped that we would get permission to go to Washington to settle our affairs with our Great Father. I visited the agent at Rock Island.[98] He was displeased because we had returned to our village, and told me that we *must* remove to the west of the Mississippi. I told him plainly that we *would not!* I visited the interpreter at his house, who advised me to do as the agent had directed me.[99] I then went to see the trader and upbraided him for buying our lands. He said that if he had not purchased them, some person else would, and that if our Great Father would make an exchange with us, he would willingly give up the land he had purchased to the government.

97. Neapope was a leading Sauk ally of Black Hawk. He urged a confederacy of Indian tribes to resist American intervention, but when none materialized he did not abandon Black Hawk as Keokuk did, but stood with him.
98. Black Hawk visited Indian agent Thomas Forsyth at Rock Island. Roger L. Nichols, *Black Hawk and the Warrior's Path* (Harlan Davidson, Inc., 1992), 65.
99. Scott Campbell was likely the interpreter referred to here.

This I thought was fair, and began to think that he had not acted as badly as I had suspected. We again repaired our lodges, and built others, as most of our village had been burnt and destroyed. Our women selected small patches to plant corn, (where the whites had not taken them within their fences,) and worked hard to raise something for our children to subsist upon.

I was told that, according to the treaty, we had no *right* to remain upon the lands *sold*, and that the government would *force* us to leave them. There was but a small portion, however, that *had been sold;* the balance remaining in the hands of the government, we claimed the right (if we had no other) to "live and hunt upon, as long as it remained the property of the government," by a stipulation in the same treaty that required us to evacuate it *after* it had been sold.[100] This was the land that we wished to inhabit, and thought we had the best right to occupy.

I heard that there was a great chief on the Wabash, and sent a party to get his advice. They informed him that we had not sold our village. He assured them, then, that if we had not sold the land on which our village stood, our Great Father would not take it from us.[101]

I started early to Malden to see the chief of my British Father, and told him my story. He gave the same reply that the chief on the Wabash had given; and in justice to him, I must say, he never gave me any bad advice: but advised me to apply to our American Father, who, he said, would do us justice. I next called on the great chief at Detroit,

100. This was the 1804 treaty. The five headmen who signed the treaty were Layauvois or Laiyurva, Pashepaho (the geiger), Quashquame (jumping fish), Outchequaka (sun fish), and Hahshequarhiqua (the bear). Kappler, "Treaty With the Sauk and Foxes, 1804," 74–77. See page 63, note 77.
101. The "great chief on the Wabash" River was William Henry Harrison.

and made the same statement to him that I had to the chief of our British Father.[102] He gave the same reply. He said, if we had not sold our lands, and would remain peaceably on them, that we would not be disturbed. This assured me that I was right, and determined me to hold out, as I had promised my people.

I returned from Malden late in the fall. My people were gone to their hunting ground, whither I followed. Here I learned that they had been badly treated all summer by the whites; and that a treaty had been held at Prairie du Chien. Ke-o-kuck and some of our people attended it, and found out that our Great Father had exchanged a small strip of the land that was ceded by Quàsh-quà-me and his party, with the Potawatomi, for a portion of their land, near Chicago; and that the object of this treaty was to get it back again; and that the United States had agreed to give them *sixteen thousand dollars a year, forever,* for this small strip of land—it being less than the twentieth part of that taken from our nation, for *one thousand dollars a year!*[103] This bears evidence of something I cannot explain. This land, they say, belonged to the United States. What reason, then, could have induced them to exchange it with the Potawatomi, if it was so valuable? Why not keep it? Or, if they found that they had made a bad bargain with the Potawatomi, why not take back their land at a fair proportion of what they gave our nation for it? If this small portion of the land that they took from us for *one thousand dollars* a year, be worth *sixteen thousand dollars a*

102. The chief of the British Father was likely British agent George Ironside Jr. The great chief at Detroit was Lewis Cass, governor of Michigan Territory.
103. Charles J. Kappler, comp. and ed., "Treaty with the Chippewa, ETC, 1829," July 29, 1829, *Indian Treaties 1778–1883* (Interland Publishing Inc., 1972), 297–300.

year forever, to the Potawatomi, then the whole tract of country taken from us ought to be worth, to our nation, *twenty times* as much as this small fraction.

Here I was again puzzled to find out how the white people reasoned; and began to doubt whether they had any standard of right and wrong!

Communication was kept up between myself and the Prophet. Runners were sent to the Arkansas, Red river and Texas—not on the subject of our lands, but a secret mission, which I am not, at present, permitted to explain.

It was related to me, that the chiefs and headmen of the Foxes had been invited to Prairie du Chien, to hold a council to settle the differences existing between them and the Sioux. That the chiefs and headmen, amounting to nine, started for the place designated, taking with them one woman—and were met by the Menominee and Sioux, near the Wisconsin and all *killed*, except one man. Having understood that the whole matter was published shortly after it occurred, and is known to the white people, I will say no more about it.

I would here remark, that our pastimes and sports had been laid aside for two years. We were a divided people, forming two parties. Ke-o-kuck being at the head of one, willing to barter our rights merely for the good opinion of the whites; and cowardly enough to desert our village to them.[104] I was at the head of the other party, and was determined to hold on to my village, although I had been *ordered* to leave it. But, I considered, as myself and band had no agency in selling our country—and that as provi-

104. Keokuk's band was sometimes called the "peace band" and he received an Arabian stallion and other gifts from the Americans for his favorable land negotiations. See, Fixico, "The Black Hawk-Keokuk Controversy," 64–78.

sion had been made in the treaty, for us all to remain on it as long as it belonged to the United States, that we could not be *forced* away. I refused, therefore, to quit my village. It was here, that I was born—and here lie the bones of many friends and relations. For this spot I felt a sacred reverence, and never could consent to leave it, without being forced therefrom.

When I called to mind the scenes of my youth, and those of later days—and reflected that the theatre on which these were acted, had been so long the home of my fathers, who now slept on the hills around it, I could not bring my mind to consent to leave this country to the whites, for any earthly consideration.

The winter passed off in gloom. We made a bad hunt, for want of the guns, traps, etc. that the whites had taken from our people for whisky! The prospect before us was a bad one. I fasted, and called upon the Great Spirit to direct my steps to the right path. I was in great sorrow—because all the whites with whom I was acquainted, and had been on terms of friendship, advised me so contrary to my wishes, that I began to doubt whether I had a *friend* among them.

Ke-o-kuck, who has a smooth tongue, and is a great speaker, was busy in persuading my band that I was wrong—and thereby making many of them dissatisfied with me. I had one consolation—for all the women were on my side, on account of their corn-fields.

On my arrival again at my village, with my band increased, I found it worse than before. I visited Rock Island. The agent again ordered me to quit my village, he said, that if we did not, troops would be sent to drive us off. He reasoned with me, and told me, it would be better for us to be with the rest of our people, so that we might avoid difficulty, and live in peace. The *interpreter* joined him, and gave me so many good reasons, that I almost wished I had not undertaken the difficult task that I had pledged myself to my brave band to perform. In this mood, I called upon the *trader*, who is fond of talking, and had long been my friend, but now amongst those advising me to give up my village. He received me very friendly, and went on to defend Ke-o-kuck in what he had done, and endeavored to show me that I was bringing distress on our women and children. He inquired, if some terms could not be made, that would be honorable to me, and satisfactory to my braves, for us to remove to the west side of the Mississippi? I replied, that if our Great Father would do us justice, and would make the proposition, I could then give up honorably. He asked me, "if the great chief at St. Louis would give us six thousand dollars to purchase provisions and other articles, if I would give up peaceably, and remove to the west side of the Mississippi?" After thinking some time, I agreed that I could honorably give up, by being paid for it, according to our customs; but told him, that I could not make the proposal myself, even if I wished, because it would be dishonorable in me to do so. He said he would do it, by sending word to the great chief at St. Louis, that he could remove us peaceably, for the amount stated, to the west side of the Mississippi. A steam-boat arrived at the island during my stay. After its departure, the *trader* told me that he had "requested a war chief, who was stationed at Galena, and was on board the steam-boat, to make the offer to the great chief at St. Louis, and that he would soon be back, and bring his answer." I did not let my people know what had taken place, for fear they would be displeased. I did not like what had been done myself, and tried to banish it from my mind.

After a few days had passed, the war chief returned, and brought for answer, that "the great chief at St. Louis would give us *nothing!*—and said if we did not remove immediately, we should be *drove off!*"[105]

I was not much displeased with the answer brought by the war chief, because I would rather have laid my bones with my forefathers than remove for any consideration. Yet if a friendly offer had been made, as I expected, I would, for the sake of my women and children, have removed peaceably.

I now resolved to remain in my village, and make no resistance, if the military came, but submit to my fate! I impressed the importance of this course on all my band, and directed them, in case the military came, not to raise an arm against them.

About this time, our agent was put out of office—for what reason, I never could ascertain.[106] I then thought, if it was for wanting to make us leave our village it was right—because I was tired of hearing him talk about it. The interpreter, who had been equally as bad in trying to persuade us to leave our village, was retained in office—and the young man who took the place of our agent, told the same old story over about removing us. I was then satisfied, that this could not have been the cause.

Our women had planted a few patches of corn, which was growing finely, and promised a subsistence for our children—but the *white people again commenced ploughing it up!* I now determined to put a stop to it, by clearing our country of the *intruders.* I went to the principal men and told them that they must and should leave our country—and gave them until the middle of the next day, to remove in. The worst left within the time appointed—but the one

105. The "great Chief at St. Louis," was William Clark.
106. Thomas Forsyth was replaced as Indian agent by Felix St. Vrain at Rock Island in 1830.

who remained, represented, that his family, (which was large,) would be in a starving condition, if he went and left his crop—and promised to behave well, if I would consent to let him remain until fall, in order to secure his crop. He spoke reasonably, and I consented.

We now resumed some of our games and pastimes—having been assured by the prophet that we would not be removed. But in a little while it was ascertained, that a great war chief, [Gen. Gaines] with a large number of soldiers, was on his way to Rock river.[107] I again called upon the prophet, who requested a little time to see into the matter. Early next morning he came to me, and said he had been *dreaming!* "That he saw nothing bad in this great war chief, [Gen. Gaines] who was now near Rock river. That the *object* of his mission was to *frighten* us from our village, that the white people might get our land for *nothing!*" He assured us that this "great war chief dare not, and would, not hurt any of us. That the Americans were at peace with the British, and when they made peace, the British required, (which the Americans agreed to,) that they should never interrupt any nation of Indians that was at peace—and that all we had to do to retain our village, was to *refuse* any, and every offer that might be made by this war chief."

The war chief arrived, and convened a council at the agency. Ke-o-kuck and Wà-pel-lo were sent for, and came with a number of their band. The council house was opened, and they were all admitted. Myself and band were then sent for to attend the council. When we arrived at the door, singing a *war song*, and armed with lances,

107. Gen. Edmund P. Gaines (1777–1849) served in the War of 1812 and commanded the US Army's Western Division at the outbreak of the Mexican-American War (1846–1848).

spears, war clubs and bows and arrows, as if going to battle, I halted, and refused to enter—as I could see no necessity or propriety in having the room crowded with those who were already there. If the council was convened for us, why have others in our room? The war chief having sent all out, except Ke-o-kuck, Wà-pel-lo, and a few of their chiefs and braves, we entered the council house in this warlike appearance, being desirous to show the war chief that we were *not afraid!* He then rose and made a speech.

He said:

"The president is very sorry to be put to the trouble and expense of sending a large body of soldiers here, to remove you from the lands you have long since ceded to the United States. Your Great Father has already warned you repeatedly, through your agent, to leave the country; and he is very sorry to find that you have disobeyed his orders. Your Great Father wishes you well: and asks nothing from you but what is reasonable and right. I hope you will consult your own interests, and leave the country you are occupying, and go to the other side of the Mississippi."

I replied: "That *we* had never sold our country. *We* never received any annuities from our American father! And *we* are determined to hold on to our village!"[108]

The war chief, apparently angry, rose and said:— "Who is *Black Hawk?* Who is *Black Hawk?*"

I responded: "I am a *Sac!* my forefather was a SAC! and all the nations call me a SAC!!"

108. The italicized "we" Patterson used here for Black Hawk's emphasis to General Gaines, suggests that Black Hawk wished to distinguish his tribe and leadership from Keokuk, and that he rejected the validity of the 1804 Treaty. J. Gerald Kennedy, ed., *Life of Black Hawk,* 105, note 68.

The war chief said:

"I came here, neither to *beg* nor *hire* you to leave your village. My business is to remove you, peaceably if I can, but *forcibly* if I must! I will now give you two days to remove in—and if you do not cross the Mississippi within that time, I will adopt measures to *force* you away!"

I told him that I never could consent to leave my village and was determined not to leave it!

The council broke up, and the war chief retired to the fort. I consulted the prophet again! He said he had been dreaming, and that the Great Spirit had directed that a woman, the daughter of Mat-ta-tas, the old chief of the village, should take a stick in her hand and go before the war chief, and tell him that she is the daughter of Mat-ta-tas, and that he had always been the *white man's friend!* That he had fought their battles—been wounded in their service—and had always spoke well of them—and she had never heard him say that he had sold their village. The whites are numerous, and can take it from us if they choose; but she hoped they would not be so unfriendly. If they were, she had one favor to ask: she wished her people to be allowed to remain long enough to gather the provisions now growing in their fields: that she was a woman, and had worked hard to raise something to support her children! And, if we are driven from our village without being allowed to save our corn, many of our little children must perish with hunger!"

Accordingly, Mat-ta-tas' daughter was sent to the fort, accompanied by several of our young men.[109] They were admitted. She went before the war chief, and told the story of the prophet! The war chief said that the president

109. This was Fort Armstrong, located five miles from Saukenuk on Rock Island.

did not send him here to make treaties with the women, nor to hold council with them![110] That our young men must leave the fort, but she might remain if she wished!

All our plans were now defeated. We must cross the river, or return to our village and await the coming of the war chief with his soldiers. We determined on the latter: but finding that our agent, interpreter, trader, and Ke-o-kuck, (who were determined on breaking my ranks,) had seduced several of my warriors to cross the Mississippi, I sent a deputation to the agent, at the request of my band, pledging myself to leave the country in the fall, provided permission was given us to remain, and secure our crop of corn, then growing—as we would be in a starving situation if we were driven off without the means of subsistence.

The deputation returned with an answer from the war chief, "that no further time would be given than that specified, and if we were not then gone, he would remove us!"

I directed my village crier to proclaim, that my orders were, in the event of the war chief coming to our village to remove us, that not a gun should be fired nor any resistance offered. That if he determined to fight, for them to remain, quietly in their lodges, and let him *kill them if he chose!*

I felt conscious that this great war chief would not hurt our people—and my object was not *war!* Had it been, we would have attacked, and killed the war chief and his braves, when in council with us—as they were then completely in our power. But his manly conduct and soldierly deportment, his mild, yet energetic manner, which proved his bravery, forbade it.

110. President Andrew Jackson.

Some of our young men who had been out as *spies,* came in and reported, that they had discovered a large body of mounted men coming towards our village, who looked like a *war party.*[111] They arrived, and took a position below Rock river, for their place of encampment. The great war chief, (Gen. Gaines,) entered Rock river in a steam-boat, with his soldiers and one big gun! They passed, and returned close by our village; but excited no alarm among my braves. No attention was paid to the boat by any of our people—even our little children, who were playing on the bank of the river, as usual, continued their amusement. The water being shallow, the boat got aground, which gave the whites some trouble. If they had asked for assistance, there was not a brave in my band, who would not willingly have aided them. Their people were permitted to pass and repass through our village, and were treated with friendship by our people.

The war chief appointed the next day to remove us! I would have remained and been taken prisoner by the *regulars,* but was afraid of the multitude *of pale faces,* who were on horseback, as they were under no restraint of their chiefs.

We crossed the Mississippi during the night, and encamped some distance below Rock Island. The great war chief convened another council, for the purpose of making a treaty with us. In this treaty he agreed to give us corn in place of that we had left growing in our fields. I touched the goose quill to this treaty, and was determined to live in peace.[112]

111. Illinois governor John Reynolds personally led state militia during Black Hawk's War, often without consulting US Army command. J. Gerald Kennedy, ed., *Life of Black Hawk,* 105, note 69.
112. The treaty was actually an agreement (not an official treaty) that reaffirmed the treaties of 1804, 1806, and 1825, but also that the Sac and Fox would stop all communications with the British.

Portrait of Black Hawk by George Catlin, 1832. He holds his medicine bag made from a black hawk and a fan made from its tail feathers. (*Smithsonian American Art Museum*)

Portrait of White Cloud by George Catlin, 1832. (*Smithsonian American Art Museum*)

Portrait of Ne-a-pope by George Catlin, 1832. (*Smithsonian American Art Museum*)

The Battle of Tippecanoe, engraving by Alonzo Chappel, 1859, New York, Johnson, Fry & Co. (*New York Public Library*)

View of the great treaty held at Prairie du Chien, September 1825, "painted on the spot by J.O. Lewis." (*Library of Congress*)

Portrait of William Clark by Charles Willson Peale, 1807. (*Independence National Historic Park*)

Robert Dickson. (*Wikimedia Commons*)

Fort Madison by Louis Henry of the Arnz and Company, 1854. (*New York Public Library*)

A view of Davenport, left, Rock Island and Fort Armstrong, center, and the town of Rock Island, right. Drawn and engraved by J. C. Wild, 1844. (*New York Public Library*)

Henry Atkinson. (*Wikimedia Commons*)

Photograph of Ke-o-kuk by Thomas Easterly, 1847. (*Missouri History Museum Collection*)

Edmund P. Gaines. (*Library of Congress*)

Henry Dodge. (*Wisconsin Historical Society*)

"Battle of Stillman's Run," from *Great Indian Chief of the West* by Benjamin Drake, 1854. (*Wikimedia Commons*)

The Battle of Bad Axe. On August 1, 1832, Black Hawk's weary and starving band reached the eastern bank of the Mississippi intending to cross the river, but the the steamboat *Warrior* intercepted them and began firing, although the Indians held up white flags of surrender. (*Wikimedia Commons*)

The Battle of Bad Axe. Early on August 2, militia and General Atkinson's men encountered part of Black Hawk's band that had yet to cross the Mississippi. The band attempted to give themselves up but many were senselessly slaughtered by the Americans. (*New York Public Library*)

Black Hawk and other prisoners painted by George Catlin during their imprisonment at Jefferson Barracks in 1832. Note the cannon balls attached to their ankles. From left to right: White Cloud; Wa-saw-me-saw (Roaring Thunder, Black Hawk's son); Black Hawk; Na-se-ús-kuk (Whirling Thunder, Black Hawk's son); Ne-a-pope; Pam-a-hó. (*National Gallery of Art*)

Top: Black Hawk and Jim Thorpe Sac and Fox Nation in Stroud, Oklahoma; center, Black Hawk Health Center Sac and Fox Nation in Stroud, Oklahoma; bottom, Black Hawk Historic Site marker, Rock Island, Illinois. (*Dr. Michelle Martin*)

The corn that had been given us, was soon found to be inadequate to our wants; when loud lamentations were heard in the camp, by our women and children, for their *roasting-ears, beans* and *squashes.* To satisfy them, a small party of braves went over, in the night, to steal corn from their own fields. They were discovered by the whites, and fired upon. Complaints were again made of the depredations committed by some of my people, *on their own cornfields!*

I understood from our agent, that there had been a provision made in one of our treaties for assistance in agriculture, and that we could have our fields ploughed if we required it. I therefore called upon him, and requested him to have me a small log house built, and a field plowed that fall, as I wished to live retired. He promised to have it done. I then went to the trader, and asked for permission to be buried in the grave-yard at our village, among my old friends and warriors; which he gave me cheerfully. I then returned to my people satisfied.

A short time after this, a party of Fox went up to Prairie du Chien to avenge the murder of their chiefs and relations, which had been committed the summer previous, by the Menominee and Sioux. When they arrived in the vicinity of the encampment of the Menominee, they met with a Winnebago, and inquired for the Menominee camp; and they requested him to go on before them and see if there were any Winnebago in it—and if so, to tell them that they had better return to their own camp. He went, and gave the information, not only to the Winnebago, but to the Menominee, that they might be prepared. The party soon followed, killed twenty-eight Menominee, and made their escape.

This retaliation, (which with us is considered lawful and right,) created considerable excitement among the whites! A demand was made for the Foxes to be surrendered to, and *tried* by, the white people! The principal men came to me during the fall, and asked my advice. I conceived that they had done right, and that our Great Father acted very *unjustly,* in demanding *them,* when he had suffered all their chiefs to be decoyed away, and *murdered* by the Menominee, without having ever made a similar demand of *them.* If he had no right in the first instance, he had none now; and for my part, I conceived the *right* very *questionable,* if not altogether usurpation, in any case, where a difference exists between two nations, for him to interfere! The Fox joined my band, with an intention to go out with them to hunt.

About this time, Ne-a-pope, (who started to Malden when it was ascertained that the great war chief, Gen. Gaines, was coming to remove us,) returned. He said he had seen the chief of our British Father, and asked him if the Americans could *force* us to leave our village? He said—"If we had not sold our village and land the American government could not take them from us. That the *right,* being vested in us, could only be transferred by the voice and *will* of the whole nation; and that, as *we* had never given our consent to the sale of our country, it remained our exclusive property—from which the American government could never force us away! and that, in the event of *war,* we should have nothing to *fear!* as they would stand by and *assist* us!"

He said he had called at the prophet's village on his way down, and had there learned, for the first time, that we had left our village.[113] He informed me, privately, that the prophet was anxious to see me, as he had much good

113. White Cloud's village was located 40 to 45 miles northeast of Saukenuk on the Rock River.

news to tell me, and that I would hear good news in the spring from our British Father. The prophet requested me to inform you of all the particulars. I would much rather, however, you should see him, and learn all from himself. But I will tell you, that he has received expresses from our British father, who says that he is going to send us guns, ammunition, provisions, and clothing, early in the spring. The vessels that bring them will come by way of Mil-wá-ke. The prophet has likewise received wampum and tobacco from the different nations on the lakes—Ottawa, Chippewa, Potawatomi; and as for the Winnebago, he has them all at his command. We are going to be happy once more!

I told him that I was pleased that our British Father intended to see us righted. That we had been driven from our lands without receiving anything for them—and I now began to hope, from his *talk,* that my people would be once more happy. If I could accomplish this, I would be satisfied. I am now growing old, and could spend the remnant of my time anywhere. But I wish first to see my people happy. I can then leave them cheerfully. This has always been my constant aim; and I now begin to hope that our sky will soon be clear.

Ne-a-pope said: "The prophet told me that all the different tribes before mentioned would *fight* for us, if necessary, and the British would support us. And, if we *should be whipped,* (which is hardly possible,) we will still be safe, the prophet having received a friendly *talk* from the chief of Wàs-sa-cum-mi-co, (at Selkirk's settlement,) telling him, that if we were not satisfied in our country, to let him know, and he would make us happy. That he had received information from our British father, that we had been badly treated by the Americans. We must go and see the prophet. I will go first; you had better remain and get as many of our people to join us as you can. You now know every thing that we have done. We leave the matter with you to arrange among your people as you please. I will return to the prophet's village tomorrow; you can, in the mean time, make up your mind as to the course you will take, and send word to the prophet by me, as he is anxious to assist us, and wishes to know whether you will join us, and assist to make your people happy!"[114]

During the night, I thought over every thing that Ne-a-pope had told me, and was pleased to think that, by a little exertion on my part, I could accomplish the object of all my wishes. I determined to follow the advice of the prophet, and sent word by Ne-a-pope, that I would get all my braves together, explain every thing that I had heard to them, and recruit as many as I could from the different villages.

Accordingly, I sent word to Ke-o-kuck's band and the Fox tribe, and explained to them all the good news I had heard. They would not hear. Ke-o-kuck said that I had been imposed upon by *liars,* and had much better remain where I was and keep quiet. When he found that I was determined to make an attempt to secure my village, and fearing that some difficulty would arise, he made application to the agent and great chief at St. Louis, for permission for the chiefs of our nation to go to Washington to see our Great Father, that we might have our difficulties

114. Another factor leading to war in 1832 was that Black Hawk and members of his band realized that not only did settlers plow the cornfields of his people, but they also plowed the graves of his people who had been buried at Saukenuk. Such desecration angered Black Hawk and those who felt the same way of wanting revenge against the settlers. To make matters worse, Illinois militiamen were reported to have dug up the graves and burned the bones of some of the dead Sauk and Fox. Nichols, *Black Hawk and the Warrior's Path,* 101.

settled amicably. Ke-o-kuck also requested the trader, who was going on to Washington, to call on our Great Father and explain everything to him, and ask for permission for us to come on and see him.[115]

Having heard nothing favorable from the great chief at St. Louis, I concluded that I had better keep my band together, and recruit as many more as possible, so that I would be prepared to make the attempt to rescue my village in the spring, provided our Great Father did not send word for us to go to Washington.

The trader returned. He said he had called on our Great Father and made a full statement to him in relation to our difficulties, and had asked leave for us to go to Washington, but had received no answer.

I had determined to listen to the advice of my friends—and if permitted to go to see our Great Father, to abide by his counsel, whatever it might be. Every overture was made by Ke-okuck to prevent difficulty, and I anxiously hoped that something would be done for my people, that it might be avoided. But there was *bad management somewhere, or the difficulty that has taken place would have been avoided.*

When it was ascertained that we would not be permitted to go to Washington, I resolved upon my course, and again tried to recruit some braves from Ke-o-kuck's band to accompany me, but could not.

Conceiving that the *peaceable disposition* of Ke-o-kuck and his people had been, in a great measure, the cause of our having been driven from our village, I ascribed their present feelings to the same cause; and immediately went to work to recruit all my own band, and made preparations

115. Interpreter and fur trader at Fort Armstrong, Antoine LeClaire would accompany Black Hawk's delegation to Washington in late April 1833.

to ascend Rock river. I made my encampment on the Mississippi, where fort Madison had stood; requested my people to rendezvous at that place, and sent out soldiers to bring in the warriors, and stationed my sentinels in a position to prevent any from moving up until *all* were ready.

My party having all come in and got ready, we commenced our march up the Mississippi—our women and children in canoes, carrying such provisions as we had, camp equipage, &c., and my braves and warriors on horseback, armed and equipped for defence.[116] The prophet came down and joined us below Rock river, having called at Rock Island on his way down, to consult the war chief, agent, and trader, who, he said, used many arguments to dissuade him from going with us; and requested him to come and meet us, and turn us back. They told him also, that there was a war chief on his way to Rock Island with a large body of soldiers.

The prophet said he would not listen to this *talk*, because no war chief dare molest us as long as we are at *peace*. That we had a right to go where we pleased peaceably; and advised me to say nothing to my braves and warriors until we encamped that night. We moved onward until we arrived at the place where Gen. Gaines had made his encampment the year before, and encamped for the

116. Black Hawk and his people's march to reclaim Saukenuk began on April 5, 1832. Although the leadership of the pro-British band of Sauks and Foxes fell to Black Hawk, he was sixty-five years old at this time. To help Black Hawk, the four recognized war leaders of Kinnekonnesaut, Menacou, Makatauauquat and Pashetowat were too young to lead a village or band as observed later by White Cloud and Quashquame. The group lacked coherence, and included about 100 Kickapoo warriors and their families. The band had about 400 warriors total, plus their families. The one common element was their anger towards both the white settlers and their tribal kinsmen who accepted removal to west of the Mississippi. Nichols, *Black Hawk and the Warrior's Path*, 105.

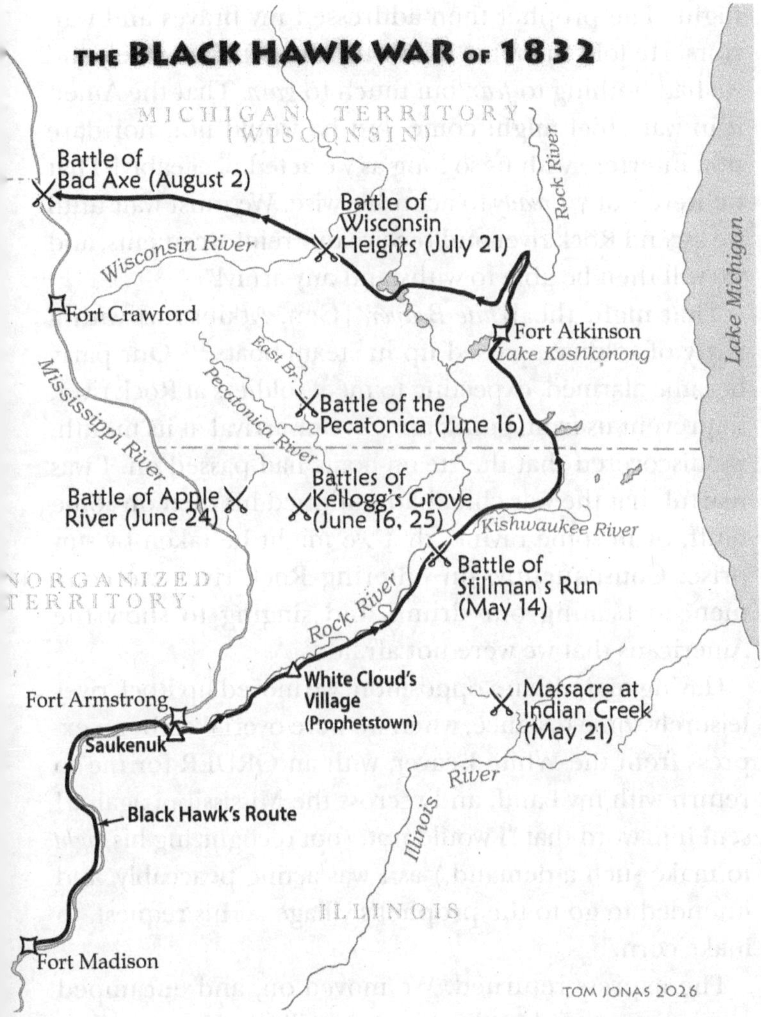
THE BLACK HAWK WAR OF 1832
MICHIGAN TERRITORY
(WISCONSIN)
Battle of Bad Axe (August 2)
Battle of Wisconsin Heights (July 21)
Rock River
Lake Michigan
Wisconsin River
Fort Crawford
Fort Atkinson
Lake Koshkonong
East Br.
Pecatonica River
Mississippi River
Battle of the Pecatonica (June 16)
Battles of Kellogg's Grove (June 16, 25)
Battle of Apple River (June 24)
Kishwaukee River
Battle of Stillman's Run (May 14)
UNORGANIZED TERRITORY
Rock River
White Cloud's Village (Prophetstown)
Fort Armstrong
Saukenuk
Massacre at Indian Creek (May 21)
River
Illinois
Black Hawk's Route
ILLINOIS
Fort Madison
TOM JONAS 2026

night. The prophet then addressed my braves and warriors. He told them to "follow us, and act like braves, and we had nothing to *fear,* but much to *gain.* That the American war chief might come, but he would not, nor dare not, interfere with us so long as we acted peaceably! That we were not *yet ready* to act otherwise. We must wait until we ascend Rock river and receive our reinforcements, and we will then be able to withstand any army!"

That night the *White Beaver,* [Gen. Atkinson,] with a party of soldiers, passed up in steam-boats.[117] Our party became alarmed, expecting to meet soldiers at Rock river, to prevent us from going up. On our arrival at its mouth, we discovered that the steam-boats had passed on. I was fearful that the war chief had stationed his men on some bluff, or in some ravine, that we might be taken by surprise. Consequently, on entering Rock river, we commenced beating our drums and singing to show the Americans that we were not afraid.

Having met with no opposition, we moved up Rock river leisurely some distance, when we were overtaken by an express from the White Beaver, with an ORDER for me to return with my band, and recross the Mississippi again. I sent him word that "I would not, (not recognizing his *right* to make such a demand,) as I was acting peaceably, and intended to go to the prophet's village, at his request, to make corn."

The express returned. We moved on, and encamped some distance below the prophet's village. Here another express came from the White Beaver, threatening to pursue us and *drive* us back, if we did not return peaceably!

117. Gen. Henry Atkinson (1782–1842) was called Wâpi-amehkwa, the "White Beaver," by the Sauk and other Indians likely because he traveled much of the time by water to negotiate treaties with the tribes. He was in overall command of US forces during the Black Hawk War.

This message roused the spirit of my band, and all were determined to remain with me and contest the ground with the war chief, should he come and attempt to drive us. We therefore directed the express to say to the war chief, "if he wished to *fight* us, he might come on!" We were determined never to be driven, and equally so, *not to make the first attack*, our object being to act only on the defensive. This we conceived our right.

Soon after the express returned, Mr. Gratiot, sub-agent for the Winnebago, with several of the chiefs and headmen of the Winnebago nation, came to our encampment.[118] He had no interpreter—and was compelled to talk through his chiefs. They said the object of his mission was, to persuade us to return. But they advised us to go on—assuring us that the further we went up Rock river the more friends we would meet, and our situation be bettered; that they were on our side, and all their people were our friends: that we must not give up—but continue to ascend Rock river, on which, in a short time, we would receive a reinforcement sufficiently strong to repulse any enemy! They said they would go down with their agent, to ascertain the strength of the enemy, and then return and give us the news: that they had to use some stratagem to *deceive* their agent, in order to *help* us!

During this council, a number of my braves hoisted the British flag, mounted their horses, and surrounded the council lodge! I discovered that the agent was very much frightened! I told one of his chiefs to tell him that he need not be alarmed—and then went out and directed my braves to desist. Every warrior immediately dismounted and returned to his lodge. After the council adjourned, I

118. Henry Gratiot (1789–1836) was a French-American farmer and miner who was one of the first settlers in Wisconsin. He remained a trusted intermediary with the Winnebago for almost ten years.

placed a sentinel at the agent's lodge, to guard him—fearing that some of my warriors might again frighten him! I had always thought that he was a good man, and was determined that he should not be hurt. He started, with his chiefs, for Rock Island.

Having ascertained that the White Beaver would not permit us to remain here, I began to consider what was best to be done, and concluded to keep up the river and see the Potawatomi, and have a talk with them. Several Winnebago chiefs were present, whom I advised of my intentions, as *they* did not seem disposed to render us any assistance. I asked them if they had not sent us *wampum* during the winter, and requested us to come and join their people and enjoy all the rights and privileges of their country? They did not deny this; and said if the white people did not interfere, they had no objection to our making corn this year, with our friend the prophet; but did not wish us to go any further up.

The next day, I started with my party to Kish-wâ-co-kee. That night I encamped a short distance above the prophet's village. After all was quiet in my camp, I sent for my chiefs, and told them that we had been *deceived!* That all the fair promises that had been held out to us, through Ne-a-pope, were *false!* But it would not do to let our party know it. We must keep it secret among ourselves—and move on to Kish-wâ-co-kee, as if all was right, and say something on the way to encourage our people. I will then call on the Potawatomi, and hear what they say, and see what they will do.

We started the next morning, after telling our people that news had just come from Mil-wâ-kee, that a chief of our British father would be there in a few days![119]

119. This may have been Robert Dickson. The British father was William IV, king of England, 1830–1837.

Finding that all our plans were defeated, I told the prophet that he must go with me, and we would see what could be done with the Potawatomi. On our arrival at Kish-wá-co-kee, an express was sent to the Potawatomi villages. The next day a deputation arrived. I inquired if they had corn in their villages? They said they had very little, and could not spare any! I asked them different questions, and received unsatisfactory answers. This talk was in the presence of all my people. I afterwards spoke to them privately, and requested them to come to my lodge after my people had got to sleep. They came, and took seats. I asked them if they had received any news from the lake from the British? They said no. I inquired if they had heard that a chief of our British father was coming to Milwá-kee, to bring us guns, ammunition, goods and provisions? They said, no! I then told them what news had been brought to me, and requested them to return to their village, and tell the chiefs that I wished to see them and have a talk with them.

After this deputation started, I concluded to tell my people, that if the White Beaver came after us, we would go back—as it was useless to think of stopping or going on without provisions. I discovered that the Winnebago and Potawatomi were not disposed to render us any assistance. The next day, the Potawatomi chiefs arrived at my camp. I had a dog killed, and made a feast.[120] When it was ready, I spread my *medicine bags*, and the chiefs began to eat. When the ceremony was about ending, I received news, that three or four hundred white men, on horseback, had been seen about eight miles off. I immediately started

120. The Sauk and Fox had an important ceremony called a Dog Feast to honor guests, and sometimes on occasion to finalize agreements; it was a spiritual and respectful event to the Creator. See page 4, note 10.

three young men, with a white flag, to meet them, and conduct them to our camp, that we might hold a council with them, and descend Rock river again. And directed them, in case the whites had *encamped*, to return, and I would go and see *them*. After this party had started, I sent five young men to see what might take place. The first party went to the encampment of the whites, and were taken prisoners. The last party had not proceeded far, before they saw about twenty men coming towards them in full gallop! They stopped, and finding that the whites were coming so fast, in a warlike attitude, they turned and retreated, but were pursued, and two of them overtaken and *killed!* The others made their escape. When they came in with the news, I was preparing my *flags* to meet the war chief. The alarm was given. Nearly all my young men were absent, about ten miles off. I started with what I had left, (about *forty*,) and had proceeded but a short distance, before we saw a part of the army approaching. I raised a yell, and said to my braves:—"Some of our people have been killed!—wantonly and cruelly murdered! We must revenge their death!"

In a little while we discovered the whole army coming towards us in full *gallop*![121] We were now confident that our first party had been killed! I immediately placed my men in front of some bushes, that we might have the first

121. The Battle of Stillman's Run, May 14, 1832, in Illinois, was also known as the Battle of Sycamore Creek and the Battle of Old Man's Creek. On May 12, 1832, Illinois Governor John Reynolds ordered Major Isaiah Stillman and his 275 militiamen with rations for four days to march from Dixon's Ferry toward Old Man's Creek to find Black Hawk and his British band to prevent hostilities. Upon discovering Stillman's camp on May 14, Black Hawk sent three braves with a white flag to set up a peace talk. It was late in the afternoon. A small group of Stillman's men rode to meet the warriors, but they panicked when

fire, when they approached close enough. They made a halt some distance from us. I gave another yell, and ordered my brave warriors to *charge* upon them—expecting that we would all be killed! They did charge! Every man rushed and fired, and the enemy *retreated!* in the utmost confusion and consternation, before my little, but brave band of warriors!

After pursuing the enemy some distance, I found it useless to follow them, as they rode so fast, and returned to my encampment with a few of my braves, (about *twenty-five* having gone in pursuit of the enemy). I lighted my pipe, and sat down to thank the Great Spirit for what we had done. I had not been long meditating, when two of the three young men I had sent out with the flag to meet the American war chief, entered! My astonishment was not greater than my joy to see them living and well. I eagerly listened to their story, which was as follows:

"When we arrived near to the encampment of the whites, a number of them rushed out to meet us, bringing their guns with them. They took us into their camp, where an American, who spoke the Sac language a little, told us that his chief wanted to know how we were—where we were going—where our camp was—and where Black Hawk was? We told him that we had come to see chief; that our chief had directed us to conduct him to our

they saw Black Hawk's scouts watching and hurried the braves into Stillman's camp. Major Stillman's and his militia attacked, but Black Hawk quickly organized his warriors to form a skirmish line using trees as cover. Discovering that they were outnumbered Stillman's attack quickly turned into a retreat to Dixon's Ferry. Within half an hour, the battle was over with a dozen militiamen dead and three to seven warriors killed. Nichols, *Black Hawk and the Warrior's Path*, 122-25 and Patrick J. Jung, *The Black Hawk War of 1832* (University of Oklahoma Press, 2007), 72-74.

camp, in case he had not encamped; and, in that event, to tell him, that he [Black Hawk,] would come to see him; he wished to hold a council with him, as he had given up all intention of going to war.

"At the conclusion of this talk, a party of white men came in, on horseback. We saw by their countenances that something had happened. A general tumult arose. They looked at us with indignation—talked among themselves for a moment—when several cocked their guns—in a second, they fired at us in the crowd; our companion fell dead! We rushed through the crowd and made our escape. We remained in ambush but a short time, before we heard yelling, like Indians running an enemy. In a little while we saw some of the whites in full speed. One of them came near us. I threw my tomahawk, and struck him on the head, which brought him to the ground! I ran to him, and *with his own knife, took off his scalp!* I took his gun, mounted his horse, and took my friend here behind me. We turned to follow our braves, who were running the enemy, and had not gone far before we overtook a white man, whose horse had mired in a swamp! My friend alighted, and tomahawked the man, who was apparently fast under his horse! He took his *scalp*, horse, and *gun!* By this time our party was some distance ahead. We followed on, and saw several white men lying dead on the way. After riding about six miles, we met our party returning. We asked them how many of our men had been killed? They said none, after the Americans retreated. We inquired then, how many whites had been killed? They replied, that they did not know; but said we will soon ascertain, as we must *scalp* them as we go back. On our return, we found *ten men*, besides the *two* we had killed before we joined our friends. Seeing that they did not yet recognize us, it being dark, we again asked, how many of our braves had been killed? They said *five!* We asked, who they were? They replied that the first party of three, who went out to meet the American war chief, had all been taken prisoners, and killed in the encampment; and that out of a party of five, who followed to see the meeting of the first party and the whites, *two* had been killed! We were now certain that they did not recognize us—nor did we tell them *who we were* until we arrived at our camp! The news of our death had reached it some time before, and all were surprised to see us again!"

The next morning I told the crier of my village to give notice that we must go and bury our dead. In a little while all were ready. A small deputation was sent for our absent warriors, and the remainder started. We first disposed of our dead, and then commenced an examination, in the enemy's deserted encampment, for plunder. We found arms; ammunition, and provisions, all which we were in want of—particularly the latter, as we were entirely without. We found, also, a variety of *saddle-bags,* (which I distributed among my braves,) and a small quantity of *whisky!* and some *little* barrels that *had* contained this *bad medicine*; but they were *empty!* I was surprised to find that the whites carried whisky with them, as I had understood that all the *pale faces* belonged to the *temperance societies!*

The enemy's encampment was in a skirt of woods near a run, about half a day's travel from Dixon's ferry. We attacked them in the prairie, with a few bushes between us, about sundown, and I expected that my whole party would be killed! I never was so much surprised, in all the fighting I have seen—knowing, too, that the Americans, generally shoot well—as I was to see this army of several hundreds, *retreating!* WITHOUT SHOWING FIGHT!! and passing immediately through their encampment. I did think that they intended to halt here, as the situation would have forbidden attack by *my party*, if *their number* had not exceeded *half mine!* as we would have been compelled to take the *open prairie*, whilst they could have *picked trees* to shield themselves from our fire!

Never was I so much surprised in my life, as I was in this attack! An army of three or four hundred, after having learned that we were sueing for *peace*, to attempt to kill the flag-bearers that had gone, unarmed, to ask for a meeting of the war chiefs of the two contending parties to hold a council, that I might return to the west side of the Mississippi, to come forward, with a full determination to demolish the few braves I had with me, to *retreat*, when they had *ten* to *one*, was unaccountable to me. It proved a different spirit from any I had ever before seen among the *pale faces!* I expected to see them fight as the Americans did with the *British* during the last war!—but they had no such braves among them!

I had resolved upon giving up the war—and sent a *flag of peace* to the American war chief—expecting, as a matter of right, reason and justice, that our *flag would be respected*, (I have always seen it so in war among the whites,) and a council convened, that we might explain our grievances, having been driven from our village the year before, without being permitted to gather the corn and provisions which our women had labored hard to cultivate, and ask for permission to return—thereby giving up all idea of going to war against the whites.

Yet, instead of this *honorable course* which *I* have always practised in war I was *forced* into WAR, with about *five hundred* warriors, to contend against *three* or *four thousand!*

The *supplies* that Ne-a-pope and the prophet told us about, and the reinforcements we were to have, were never more heard of; (and it is but justice to our British father to say, *were never promised—his chief having sent word in lieu of the lies that were brought to me,* "FOR US TO REMAIN AT **PEACE**, AS WE COULD ACCOMPLISH NOTHING BUT OUR OWN **RUIN**, BY GOING TO **WAR**!")

What was now to be done? It was worse than folly to turn back and meet an enemy where the odds was so much against us—and thereby sacrifice ourselves, our wives and children, to the fury of an enemy who had *murdered* some of our brave and *unarmed* warriors, when they were on a mission to *sue for peace!*

Having returned to our encampment, and found that all our young men had come in, I sent out *spies*, to watch the movement of the army, and commenced moving up Kish-wá-co-kee, with the balance of my people. I did not know where to go to find a place of safety for my women and children, but expected to find a good harbor about the head of Rock river. I concluded to go there—and thought my best route would be to go round the head of Kish-wá-co-kee, so that the Americans would have some difficulty, if they attempted to follow us.

On arriving at the head of Kish-wá-co-kee, I was met by a party of Winnebago, who seemed to rejoice at our success. They said they had come to offer their services, and were anxious to join us. I asked them if they knew where there was a safe place for my women and children. They told me that they would send two old men with us to guide us to a good and safe place.

I arranged war parties to send out in different directions, before I proceeded further. The Winnebagoes went alone. The war parties having all been fitted out and started, we commenced moving to the *Four Lakes*, the place where our guides were to conduct us. We had not gone far, before six Winnebagoes came in with *one scalp!* They said they had killed a man at a grove, on the road from Dixon's to the lead mines. Four days after, the party of Winnebagoes had gone out from the head of Kish-wá-co-kee, overtook us, and told me that they had killed four men, and taken their scalps; and that one of them was Ke-o-kuck's father, (the agent).[122] They proposed to have a dance over their scalps! I told them that I could have no dancing in my camp, in consequence of my having lost three young braves; but they might dance in their own camp—which they did.

Two days after, we arrived in safety at the place where the Winnebagoes had directed us. In a few days a great number of our warriors came in. I called them all around me, and addressed them. I told them, "Now is the time, if any of you wish to come into distinction, and be honored with the medicine bag! Now is the time to show your courage and bravery, and avenge the murder of our three braves!"

Several small parties went out, and returned again in a few days, with success—bringing in provision for our people. In the mean time, some *spies* came in, and reported that the army had fallen back to Dixon's ferry; and others brought news that the horsemen had broken up their camp, disbanded, and returned home.

Finding that all was safe, I made a *dog feast*, preparatory to leaving my camp with a large party, (as the enemy were stationed so far off.) Before my braves commenced feasting, I took my *medicine bags*, and addressed them in the following language:

"*Braves and Warriors:*—These are the medicine bags of our forefather, Muk-a-tà-quet, who was the father of the Sac nation. They were handed down to the great war chief of our nation, Na-ná-ma-kee, who has been at war with all

122. Agent Felix St. Vrain had been carrying a message from Gen. Atkinson to Henry Gratiot on Rock Island when his party was attacked. J. Gerald Kennedy, *Life of Black Hawk*, 107, note 77.

the nations of the lakes and all the nations of the plains, and have never yet been disgraced! I expect you all to protect them!"

After the ceremony was over, and our feasting done, I started with about two hundred warriors, following my great medicine bags! I directed my course towards sunset, and dreamed, the second night after we started, that there was a great feast for us after one day's travel! I told my warriors my dreaming in the morning, and we all started for Mos-co-ho-y-nak, [Apple river]. When we arrived in the vicinity of a fort the white people had built there, we saw four men on horseback.[123] One of my braves fired and wounded a man, when the others set up a yell, as if a large force were near and ready to come against us. We concealed ourselves, and remained in this position for some time, watching to see the enemy approach—but none came. The four men, in the mean time, ran to the fort and gave the alarm. We followed them, and attacked their fort! One of the braves, who seemed more valiant than the rest, raised his head above the picketing to fire at us, when one of my braves, with a well directed shot, put an end to his bravery! Finding that these people could not all be killed, without setting fire to their houses and fort, I thought it more prudent to be content with what flour, provisions, cattle and horses we could find, than to set fire to their buildings, as the light would be seen at a distance, and the army might suppose that we were in the neighborhood, and come upon us with a force too strong. Accordingly, we opened a house and filled our bags with flour and provisions—took several horses, and drove off some of their cattle.

123. The Apple River Fort in northern Illinois.

We started in a direction towards sunrise. After marching a considerable time, I discovered some white men coming toward us. I told my braves that we would get into the woods and kill them when they approached. We concealed ourselves until they came near enough, and then commenced yelling and firing, and made a rush upon them. About this time, their chief, with a party of men, rushed up to rescue the men we had fired upon. In a little while they commenced retreating, and left their chief and a few braves, who seemed willing and anxious to fight! They acted like *braves*, but were forced to give way when I rushed upon them with my braves. In a short time the chief returned with a larger party. He seemed determined to fight, and anxious for a battle! When he came near enough, I raised the yell, and firing commenced from both sides. The chief (who seemed to be a small man) addressed his warriors in a loud voice; but they soon retreated, leaving him and a few braves on the battle-field.[124] A great number of my warriors pursued the retreating party, and killed a number of their horses as they ran. The chief and his few braves were unwilling to leave the field. I ordered my braves to rush upon them, and had the mortification of seeing two of my *chiefs* killed, before the enemy retreated.

124. The militia commander was Capt. Clack Stone in the Battle of Apple River Fort on June 24, 1832. Moving westward, the British band arrived at Apple River Fort in the afternoon with the intention to attack the garrison of about thirty-six Illinois militia with women and children inside. Black Hawk and a force of about 200 warriors commenced the attack that lasted about forty-five minutes with neither side winning. The warriors killed only one volunteer but lost several of their own. Black Hawk's men seized all the horses from local homes, about thirty cattle, and some hogs. Patrick J. Jung, *The Black Hawk War of 1832* (University of Oklahoma Press, 2007), 113-14.

This young chief deserves great praise for his courage and bravery; but fortunately for us, his army was not all composed of such brave men! [125]

During this attack, we killed several men and about forty horses, and lost two young chiefs and seven warriors. My braves were anxious to pursue them to the fort, attack and burn it. But I told them that it was useless to waste our powder, as there was no possible chance of success if we did attack them—and that, as we had run the bear into his hole, we would there leave him, and return to our camp.

On arriving at our encampment, we found that several parties of our *spies* had returned, bringing intelligence that the army had commenced moving. Another party of *five* came in and said they had been pursued for several hours, and were attacked by twenty-five or thirty whites in

125. This was the second Battle of Kellogg's Grove, June 18, 1832. Black Hawk's band headed for Lake Koshkonong when it discovered a small scouting party of militia about a mile and a half from Kellogg's Grove. Black Hawk ordered his warriors to hide in a thicket to ambush the militiamen. The scouting party saw some of the warriors at a distance and decided to pursue them, but rode into the ambush. Two men were killed. The warriors pursued the party to the fort at Kellogg's Grove that consisted of a three-room sturdy cabin with no stockade. The warriors managed to kill three men, while some 140 volunteers crowded into the cabin that had reinforced walls. Black Hawk ordered his warriors to save their ammunition, although they killed about thirty-two horses and wounded about fifteen. The departure of the Indians ended the second Battle of Kellogg's Grove. The "young chief" in charge of the militia was Major John Dement. The first battle occurred nine days earlier when forty-three militiamen pursued and killed four of Black Hawk's braves, while losing one Illinois volunteer. In an ambush near the fort, thirty warriors killed two volunteers, the fighting stopped when the leader of the Indian war party was fatally shot. Patrick J. Jung, *The Black Hawk War of 1832* (University of Oklahoma Press, 2007), 121-23.

the woods; that the whites rushed in upon them, as they lay concealed, and received their fire, without seeing them. They immediately retreated, whilst we reloaded. They entered the thicket again, and as soon as they came near enough, we fired! Again they retreated, and again they rushed into the thicket and fired! We returned their fire, and a skirmish ensued between two of their men and one of ours, who was killed by having his throat cut! This was the only man we lost. The enemy having had three killed, they again retreated.

Another party of three Sacs had come in, and brought in two young white squaws, whom they had given to the Winnebago, to take to the whites. They said they had joined a party of Potawatomi, and went with them as a war party, against the settlers on the Illinois.

The leader of this party, a Potawatomi, had been severely whipped by this settler, some time before, and was anxious to avenge the insult and injury. While the party was preparing to start, a young Potawatomi went to the settler's house, and told him to leave it—that a war party was coming to murder them. They started, but soon returned again, as it appeared that they were all there when the war party arrived! The Potawatomi killed the whole family, except two young squaws, whom the Sacs took up on their horses, and carried off, to save their lives.—They were brought to our encampment, and a messenger sent to the Winnebago, as they were *friendly on both sides*, to come and get them, and carry them to the whites. If these young men belonging to my band, had not gone with the Potawatomi, the two young squaws would have shared the same fate as their friends.

During our encampment at the Four Lakes, we were hard put to, to obtain enough to eat to support nature. Situate[d] in a swampy, marshy country, (which had been selected in consequence of the great difficulty required to gain access thereto,) there was but little game of any sort to be found—and fish were equally scarce. The great distance to any settlement, and the impossibility of bringing supplies therefrom, if any could have been obtained, deterred our young men from making further attempts. We were forced to dig *roots* and *bark trees*, to obtain something to satisfy hunger and keep us alive! Several of our old people became so much reduced, as actually to *die with hunger!* And, finding that the army had commenced moving, and fearing that they might come upon and surround our encampment, I concluded to remove my women and children across the Mississippi, that they might return to the Sac nation again. Accordingly, on the next day, we commenced moving, with five Winnebago acting as our guides, intending to descend the Wisconsin.

Ne-a-pope, with a party of twenty, remained in our rear, to watch for the enemy, whilst we were proceeding to the Wisconsin, with our women and children. We arrived, and had commenced crossing them to an island, when we discovered a large body of enemy coming towards us. We were now compelled to fight, or sacrifice our wives and children to the fury of the whites! I met them with fifty warriors, (having left the balance to assist our women and children in crossing,) about a mile from the river, when an attack immediately commenced. I was mounted on a fine horse, and was pleased to see my warriors so brave. I addressed them in a loud voice, telling them to stand their ground, and never yield it to the enemy. At this time I was on the rise of a hill, where I wished to form my warriors, that we might have some advantage over the whites. But the enemy succeeded in gaining this point, which compelled us to fall back into a deep ravine, from which we continued firing at them and they at us, until it began to grow dark. My horse having been wounded twice during this engagement, and fearing from his loss of blood, that he would soon give out—and finding that the enemy would not come near enough to receive our fire, in the dusk of the evening—and knowing that our women and children had had sufficient time to reach the island in the Wisconsin, I ordered my warriors to return, in different routes, and meet me at the Wisconsin—and were astonished to find that the enemy were not disposed to pursue us.[126]

In this skirmish, with fifty braves, I defended and accomplished my passage over the Wisconsin, with a loss of only six men; though opposed by a host of mounted militia. I would not have fought there, but to gain time for my women and children to cross to an island. A warrior will duly appreciate the embarrassments I labored under—and whatever may be the sentiments of the *white people*, in relation to this battle, my nation, though fallen, will award to me the reputation of a great brave, in conducting it.

The loss of the enemy could not be ascertained by our party; but I am of opinion, that it was much greater, in proportion, than mine. We returned to the Wisconsin, and crossed over to our people.

126. This was the Battle of Wisconsin Heights, July 21, 1832. Sixty-eight warriors of Black Hawk were killed by 750 militiamen. Black Hawk's band proceeded westward to cross the Wisconsin River when the rearguard of the band was attacked by militiamen. Black Hawk had assumed that Napope was leading the rearguard to help protect the main body of the band to cross the river. Instead, White Cloud had sent Napope out with a hunting party that could not rejoin the band due to the militiamen. Frustrated, Black Hawk took charge of the rearguard consisting of about fifty Sauk warriors and about seventy Kickapoo warriors. Firing from hilltops, the rearguard succeeded in holding off the enemy for the main part of the band to cross, with the rearguard immediately following them. Patrick J. Jung, *The Black Hawk War of 1832* (University of Oklahoma Press, 2007),153-54.

Here some of my people left me, and descended the Wisconsin, hoping to escape to the west side of the Mississippi, that they might return home. I had no objection to their leaving me, as my people were all in a desperate condition—being worn out with travelling, and starving from hunger. Our only hope to save ourselves, was to get across the Mississippi. But few of this party escaped. Unfortunately for them, a party of soldiers from Prairie du Chien, was stationed on the Wisconsin, a short distance from its mouth, who fired upon our distressed people. Some were killed, others drowned, several taken prisoners, and the balance escaped to the woods and perished with hunger. Among this party were a great many women and children.

I was astonished to find that Ne-a-pope and his party of *spies* had not yet come in—they having been left in my rear to bring the news, if the enemy were discovered. It appeared, however, that the whites had come in a different direction, and intercepted our trail but a short distance from the place where we first saw them—leaving our spies considerably in the rear. Ne-a-pope, and one other, retired to the Winnebago village, and there remained during the war! The balance of his party, being *brave men*, and considering our interest as their own, returned, and joined our ranks.

Myself and band having no means to descend the Wisconsin, I started, over a rugged country, to go to the Mississippi, intending to cross it, and return to my nation. Many of our people were compelled to go on foot, for want of horses, which, in consequence of their having had nothing to eat for a long time, caused our march to be very slow. At length we arrived at the Mississippi, having lost some of our old men and little children, who perished on the way with hunger.

We had been here but a little while, before we saw a steam boat (the "Warrior,") coming. I told my braves not to shoot, as I intended going on board, so that we might save our women and children. I knew the captain [Throckmorton], and was determined to give myself up to him. I then sent for my *white flag*. While the messenger was gone, I took a small piece of white cotton, and put it on a pole, and called to the captain of the boat, and told him to send his little canoe ashore, and let me come on board. The people on the boat asked whether we were Sac or Winnebago. I told a Winnebago to tell them that we were Sac, and wanted to give ourselves up! A Winnebago on the boat called to us "*to run and hide, that the whites were going to shoot!*" About this time one of my braves had jumped into the river, bearing a white flag to the boat—when another sprang in after him, and brought him to shore. The firing then commenced from the boat, which was returned by my braves, and continued for some time. Very few of my people were hurt after the first fire, having succeeded in getting behind old logs and trees, which shielded them from the enemy's fire.[127]

The Winnebago, on the steam boat, must either have misunderstood what was told, or did not tell it to the captain correctly; because I am confident that he would not have fired upon us, if he had known my wishes. I have always considered him a good man, and too great a brave to fire upon an enemy when sueing for quarters.

After the boat left us, I told my people to cross, if they could, and wished; that I intended going into the

127. The captain was Joseph Throckmorton (1800–1872), an American steamboat builder who was well known along the upper Mississippi River. According to Throckmorton, he thought the white flag was a ruse. J. Gerald Kennedy, *Life of Black Hawk*, 107, note 83.

Chippewa country. Some commenced crossing, and such as had determined to follow them, remained—only three lodges going with me. Next morning, at daybreak, a young man overtook me, and said that all my party had determined to cross the Mississippi—that a number had already got over safe, and that he had heard the white army last night within a few miles of them. I now began to fear that the whites would come up with my people, and kill them, before they could get across. I had determined to go and join the Chippewa; but reflecting that by this I could only save myself, I concluded to return, and die with my people, if the Great Spirit would not give us another victory! During our stay in the thicket, a party of whites came close by us, but passed on without discovering us!

Early in the morning a party of whites, being in advance of the army, came upon our people, who were attempting to cross the Mississippi. They tried to give themselves up—the whites paid no attention to their entreaties—but commenced *slaughtering* them! In a little while the whole army arrived. Our braves, but few in number, finding that the enemy paid no regard to age or sex, and seeing that they were murdering helpless women and little children, determined to *fight until they were killed!* As many women as could, commenced swimming the Mississippi, with their children on their backs. A number of them were drowned, and some shot, before they could reach the opposite shore.

One of my braves, who gave me this information, piled up some saddles before him, (when the fight commenced,) to shield himself from the enemy's fire, and killed three white men! But seeing that the whites were coming too close to him, he crawled to the bank of the river, without being perceived, and hid himself under it, until the enemy retired. He then came to me and told me what had been done.[128] After hearing this sorrowful news, I started, with my little party, to the Winnebago village at Prairie La Cross. On my arrival there, I entered the lodge of one of the chiefs, and told him that I wished him to go with me to his father—that I intended to give myself up to the American war chief, and *die*, if the Great Spirit saw proper! He said he would go with me. I then took my *medicine bag*, and addressed the chief. I told him that it was "the soul of the Sac nation—that it never had been dishonored in any battle—take it, it is my life—dearer than life—and give it to the American chief!" He said he would keep it, and take care of it, and if I was suffered to live, he would send it to me.

During my stay at the village, the squaws made me a white dress of deer skin. I then started, with several Winnebago, and went to their agent, at Prairie de Chien, and gave myself up.[129]

On my arrival there, I found to my sorrow, that a large body of Sioux had pursued, and killed, a number of our

128. This was the Battle of Bad Axe River, August 2, 1832. It lasted for two days starting on August 1. Although the battle started on August 1, with soldiers from the steamboat "Warrior" firing at the British band on the east bank of the Mississippi and killing twenty-three Indians. One soldier was wounded. Roughly ten miles to the east, General Henry Atkinson and his soldiers camped. At 6:00 a.m. on August 2, Atkinson's army marched in the right direction when eleven bodies were found because the Indians had starved to death. That morning about 200 of Black Hawk's band crossed the Mississippi, while 110 drowned or died in the river. By 2:00 p.m. the massacre was over. A total of about 150 were killed, and 75 were taken as prisoners, including Black Hawk. Only five soldiers were killed and about twenty were wounded. Patrick J. Jung, *The Black Hawk War of 1832* (University of Oklahoma Press, 2007),166-72.
129. Black Hawk, along with White Cloud, surrendered to Gen. Joseph M. Street, US agent to the Winnebago, on August 27, 1832.

women and children, who had got safely across the Mississippi. The whites ought not to have permitted such conduct—and none but *cowards* would ever have been guilty of such cruelty—which has always been practised on our nation by the Sioux.

The massacre, which terminated the war, lasted about two hours. Our loss in killed, was about sixty, besides a number that were drowned. The loss of the enemy could not be ascertained by my braves, exactly; but they think that they killed about *sixteen*, during the action.

I was now given up by the agent to the commanding officer at fort Crawford, (the White Beaver having gone down the river.) We remained here a short time, and then started to Jefferson Barracks, in a steam-boat, under the charge of a young war chief [Lt. Jefferson Davis], who treated us all with much kindness.[130] He is a good and brave young chief, with whose conduct I was much pleased. On our way down, we called at Galena, and remained a short time. The people crowded to the boat to see us; but the war chief would not permit them to enter the apartment where we were—knowing from what his own feelings would have been, if he had been placed in a similar situation, that we did not wish to have a gaping crowd around us.

We passed Rock Island, without stopping. The great war chief [Gen. Scott,] who was then at fort Armstrong, came out in a small boat to see us; but the captain of the steam boat would not allow any body from the fort to come on

130. Jefferson Davis (1808–1889) escorted Black Hawk and the rest of the prisoners of war to Jefferson Barracks near St. Louis in early September 1832. In late April 1833, Davis would escort Black Hawk and other Sauk prisoners to Washington, DC. Davis became a US senator of Mississippi, and after the state seceded from the Union, he would be elected president of the Confederate States of America in 1861.

board of his boat, in consequence of the cholera raging among the soldiers. I did think the captain ought to have permitted the war chief to come on board to see me, because I could see no danger to be apprehended by it. The war chief looked well, and I have since heard, was constantly among his soldiers, who were sick and dying, administering to their wants, and had not caught the disease from them—and I thought it absurd to think that any of the people on the steam boat, could be afraid of catching the disease from a *well* man. But these people have not got bravery like war chiefs, who never *fear* any thing![131]

On our way down, I surveyed the country that had cost us so much trouble, anxiety, and blood, and that now caused me to be a prisoner of war. I reflected upon the ingratitude of the whites, when I saw their fine houses, rich harvests, and every thing desirable around them; and recollected that all this land had been ours, for which me and my people had never received a dollar, and that the

131. When General Henry Atkinson and his men had trouble finding Black Hawk and his band, President Jackson sent an order to General Winfield Scott (1786–1866) to go to the Wisconsin area to find Black Hawk. A cholera outbreak delayed Scott getting to Illinois, and the final battle at Bad Axe had occurred before he arrived. Scott and Illinois Governor John Reynolds negotiated the Sauk Treaty of 1832 with Keokuk that officially ended the Black Hawk War. Called by some people "Old Fuss and Feathers," for insisting on proper military dress, Scott served as commanding general of the U.S. Army under seven presidents from 1841 to 1861. In his memoirs he summed up the Battle of Bad Axe: "on arriving at Prairie du Chien [Fort Crawford], was glad to find that [General] Atkinson, after a most fagging march of weeks and hundreds of miles, following the devious retreat of the Hawk, finally overtook him at the mouth of the Badaxe in the act of crossing the Mississippi, with his band, and in a gallant combat, killed many of his followers, made others prisoners, and dispersed the remainder." *Memoirs of Winfield Scott* (Sheldon & Co., 1864), 122.

whites were not satisfied until they took our village and our grave-yards from us, and removed us across the Mississippi.

On our arrival at Jefferson barracks, we met the great war chief [White Beaver,] who had commanded the American army against my little band. I felt the humiliation of my situation: a little while before, I had been the leader of my braves, now I was a prisoner of war! but had surrendered myself. He received us kindly, and treated us well.

We are now confined to the barracks, and forced to wear the *ball and chain!* This was extremely mortifying, and altogether useless. Was the White Beaver afraid that I would break out of his barracks, and run away? Or was he ordered to inflict this punishment upon me? If I had taken him prisoner on the field of battle, I would not have wounded his feelings so much, by such treatment—knowing that a brave war chief would prefer *death to dishonor!* But I do not blame the White Beaver for the course he pursued—it is the custom among white soldiers, and, I suppose, was a part of his duty.

The time dragged heavily and gloomily along throughout the winter, although the White Beaver done every thing in his power to render us comfortable. Having been accustomed, throughout a long life, to roam the forests o'er—to go and come at liberty—confinement, and under such circumstances, could not been less than torture!

We passed away the time making pipes, until spring, when we were visited by the agent, trader, and interpreter, from Rock Island, Ke-o-kuck, and several chiefs and braves of our nation, and my wife and daughter. I was rejoiced to see the two latter, and spent my time very agreeable with them and my people, as long as they remained.

The trader presented me with some dried venison, which had been killed and cured by some of my friends.

This was a valuable present; and although he had given me many before, none ever pleased me so much. This was the first meat I had eaten for a long time, that reminded me of the former pleasures of my own wigwam, which had always been stored with plenty.

Ke-o-kuck and his chiefs, during their stay at the barracks, petitioned our Great Father, the president, to release us; and pledged themselves for our good conduct.[132] Now began to hope that I would soon be restored to liberty, and the enjoyment of my family and friends; having heard that Ke-o-kuck stood high in the estimation of our Great Father, because he did not join me in the war. But I was soon disappointed in my hopes. An order came from our Great Father to the White Beaver, to send us on to Washington.

In a little while all were ready, and left Jefferson barracks on board of a steam boat, under charge of a young war chief, whom the White Beaver sent along as a guide to Washington.[133] He carried with him an interpreter and one soldier. On our way up the Ohio, we passed several large villages, the names of which were explained to me. The first is called Louisville, and is a very pretty village, situate[d] on the bank of the Ohio river. The next is Cincinnati, which stands on the bank of the same river.

132. Andrew Jackson was the US president from 1829 to 1837. On September 21, 1832, the Sac and Fox signed a treaty with the United States known as the "Corn Treaty" because article ten provided six thousand bushels of corn, including beef, pork, salt, and flour. Kappler, *Indian Treaties 1778-1883* (Interland Publishing Inc., 1972), 349–51.
133. Black Hawk's visit to Washington, DC, and other eastern cities began in April 1833, consisting of Black Hawk, his son Nasheaskuk, the prophet White Cloud, and several noted leaders of Black Hawk's band. All were escorted by Lt. Jefferson Davis until Major John Garland took over the remainder of the trip. Jung, *The Black Hawk War of 1832*, 194.

This is a large and beautiful village, and seemed to be in a thriving condition. The people gathered on the bank as we passed, in great crowds, apparently anxious to see us.

On our arrival at Wheeling, the streets and river's banks were crowded with people, who flocked from every direction to see us. While we remained here, many called upon us, and treated us with kindness—no one offering to molest or misuse us. This village is not so large as either of those before mentioned, but is quite a pretty village.

We left the steam boat here, having travelled a long distance on the prettiest river (except our Mississippi,) that I ever saw—and took the stage. Being unaccustomed to this mode of travelling, we soon got tired, and wished ourselves seated in a canoe on one of our own rivers, that we might return to our friends. We had travelled but a short distance, before our carriage turned over, from which I received a slight injury, and the soldier had one arm broken. I was sorry for this accident, as the young man had behaved well.

We had a rough and mountainous country for several days, but had a good trail for our carriage. It is astonishing to see what labor and pains the white people have had to make this road, as it passes over an immense number of mountains, which are generally covered with rocks and timber; yet it has been made smooth, and easy to travel upon.

Rough and mountainous as is this country, there are many wigwams and small villages standing on the road side. I could see nothing in the country to induce the people to live in it; and was astonished to find so many whites living on the hills!

I have often thought of them since my return to my own people; and am happy to think that they prefer living in their *own* country, to coming out to *ours*, and driving us from it that they might live upon and enjoy it—as many of the whites have already done. I think, with them, that wherever the Great Spirit places his people, they ought to be satisfied to remain, and thankful for what He has given them; and not drive others from the country. He has given them, because it happens to be better than theirs! This is contrary to our way of thinking; and from my intercourse with the whites, I have learned that one great principle of *their religion* is, "to do unto others as you wish them to do unto you!" Those people in the mountains seem to act upon this principle; but the settlers on our frontiers and on our lands, seem never to think of it, if we are to judge by their actions.

The first village of importance that we came to, after leaving the mountains, is called Hagerstown.[134] It is a large village to be so far from a river, and is very pretty. The people appear to live well, and enjoy themselves much.

We passed through several small villages on the way to Fredericktown, but I have forgotten their names. This last is a large and beautiful village. The people treated us well, as they did at all the other villages where we stopped.

Here we came to another road, much more wonderful than that through the mountains. They call it a *rail road!* I examined it carefully, but need not describe it, as the whites know all about it. It is the most astonishing sight I ever saw. The great road over the mountains will bear no comparison to it—although it has given the white people much trouble to make. I was surprised to see so much labor and money expended to make a good road for easy travelling. I prefer riding on horseback, however, to any other way; but suppose that these people would not have

134. Hagerstown, Maryland, was founded in 1762 and renamed in 1813.

gone to so much trouble and expense to make a road, if they did not prefer riding in their new fashioned carriages, which seem to run without any trouble. They certainly deserve great praise for their industry.

On our arrival at Washington, we called to see our Great Father, the President. He looks as if he had seen many winters as I have, and seems to be a *great brave!*[135] I had very little talk with him, as he appeared to be busy, and did not seem much disposed to talk. I think he is a good man; and although he talked but little, he treated us very well. His wigwam is well furnished with every thing good and pretty, and is very strongly built.

He said he wished to know the *cause* of my going to war against his white children. I thought he ought to have known this before; and, consequently, said but little to him about it—as I expected he knew as well as I could tell him.

He said he wanted us to go to fortress Monroe, and stay awhile with the war chief who commanded it.[136] But, having been so long from my people, I told him that I would rather return to my nation—that Ke-o-kuck had come here once on a visit to see him, as we had done, and he let him return again, as soon as he wished; and that I expected to be treated in the same way. He insisted, however, on our going to fortress Monroe; and as our interpreter could not understand enough of our language to interpret a speech, I concluded it was best to obey our Great Father, and say nothing contrary to his wishes.

135. In late April 1833 during Black Hawk's visit President Andrew Jackson was sixty-six years old. Both Black Hawk and Jackson were born in 1767.
136. Colonel Abraham Eustis (1786–1843) was the commander at Fort Monroe, Virginia. Black Hawk remained at Fort Monroe for five months. While confined he sat for a number of portraits, including that of Charles Bird King.

During our stay at the city, we were called upon by many of the people, who treated us well, particularly the squaws! We visited the great *council house* of the Americans—the place where they keep their *big guns*—and all the public buildings, and then started to fortress Monroe. The war chief met us on our arrival, and shook hands, and appeared glad to see me. He treated us with great friendship, and talked to me frequently. Previous to our leaving this fort, he gave us a feast, and made us some presents, which I intend to keep for his sake. He is a very good man, and a great *brave!* I was sorry to leave him, although I was going to return to my people, because he had treated me like a brother, during all the time I remained with him.

Having got a new guide, a war chief [Maj. Garland,] we started for our own country, taking a circuitous route. Our Great Father being about to pay a visit to his children in the *big towns* towards sunrising, and being desirous that we should have an opportunity of seeing them, directed our guide to take us through.

On our arrival at Baltimore, we were much astonished to see so large a village; but the war chief told us that we would soon see a *larger one.* This surprised us more. During our stay here, we visited all the public buildings and places of amusement—saw much to admire, and were well entertained by the people, who crowded to see us. Our Great Father was there at the same time, and seemed to be much liked by his white children, who flocked around him, (as they had done us,) to shake him by the hand. He did not remain long—having left the city before us.

We left Baltimore in a steam boat, and travelled in this way to the big village, where they make *medals* and *money* [Philadelphia]. We again expressed surprise at finding this village so much larger than the one we had left; but the war chief again told us, that we would soon see another much larger than this. I had no idea that the white people had such large villages, and so many people. They were very kind to us—showed us all their great public works, their ships and steam boats. We visited the place where they make money [the mint], and saw the men engaged at it. They presented each of us with a number of pieces of the *coin* as they fell from the mint, which are very handsome.

I witnessed a militia training in this city, in which were performed a number of singular military feats. The chiefs and men were well dressed, and exhibited quite a warlike appearance. I think our system of military parade far better than that of the whites—but, as I am now done going to war, I will not describe it, or say any thing more about war, or the preparations necessary for it.

We next started to New York, and on our arrival near the wharf, saw a large collection of people gathered at Castle-Garden. We had seen many wonderful sights in our way—large villages, the great *national road* over the mountains, the *rail roads*, steam carriages, ships, steam boats, and many other things; but we were now about to witness a sight more surprising than any of these. We were told that a man was going up into the air in a balloon![137] We watched with anxiety to see if it could be true; and to our utter astonishment, saw him ascend in the air until the eye could no longer perceive him. Our people were all surprised, and one of our young men asked the *prophet* if he was going up to see the Great Spirit?

After the ascension of the balloon, we landed, and got into a carriage, to go to the house that had been provided

137. The first manned balloon flight in the United States took place in Philadelphia on January 9, 1793. Charles Ferson Durant made the first professional balloon flight in New York in September 1830 from Battery Park.

for our reception. We had proceeded but a short distance, before the street was so crowded that it was impossible for the carriage to pass. The war chief then directed the coachman to take another street, and stop at a different house from the one he had intended. On our arrival here, we were waited upon by a number of gentlemen, who seemed much pleased to see us. We were furnished with good rooms, good provisions, and every thing necessary for our comfort.

The chiefs of this *big village*, being desirous that all their people should have an opportunity to see us, fitted up their great *council house* for this purpose, where we saw an immense number of people; all of whom treated us with friendship, and many with great generosity. One of their great chiefs, John A. Graham, waited upon us and made a very pretty talk, which appeared in the village papers, one of which I now hand you.[138]

"BROTHERS: Open your ears. You are brave men. You have fought like tigers, but in a bad cause. We have conquered you. We were sorry last year that you raised the tomahawk against us; but we believe you did not know us then as you do now. We think, in time to come, you will be wise, and that we shall be friends forever. You see that we are a great people, numerous as the flowers of the field, as the shells on the sea shore, or the fishes in the sea.

"We put one hand on the eastern, and at the same time the other on the western ocean. We all act together. If some time our great men talk long and loud at our council fires, but shed one drop of white men's blood, our young warriors, as thick as the stars of the night, will leap aboard of our great boats, which fly on the waves and over

138. The following four paragraphs of Mr. Graham's Speech are from the 1882 edition of Black Hawk's autobiography.

the lakes—swift as the eagle in the air—then penetrate the woods, make the big guns thunder, and the whole heavens red with the flames of the dwellings of their enemies. Brothers, the President has made you a great talk. He has but one mouth. That one has sounded the sentiments of all the people. Listen to what he has said to you. Write it on your memories, it is good, very good.

"Black hawk, take these jewels, a pair of topaz earrings, beautifully set in gold, for your wife or daughter as a token of friendship, keeping in mind, that women and children are the favorites of the Great Spirit. These jewels are from an old man, whose head is whitened with the snows of seventy winters, an old man who has thrown down his bow, put off his sword, and now stands leaning on his staff, waiting the commands of the Great Spirit. Look around you, see all this mighty people, then go to your homes, open your arms to receive your families. Tell them to buy the hatchet, to make bright the chain of friendship, to love the white men, and to live in peace with them, as long as the rivers run into the sea, and the sun rises and sets. If you do so, you will be happy. You will then insure [ensure] the prosperity of unborn generations of your tribes, who will go hand in hand with the sons of the white men, and all shall be blessed by the Great Spirit. Peace and happiness by the blessing of the Great Spirit attend you. Farewell."

In reply to this fine talk, I said, "Brother: We like your talk. We like the white people. They are very kind to us. We shall not forget it. Your council is good. We shall attend to it. Your valuable present shall go to my squaw. We shall always be friends."

The chiefs were particular in showing us every thing that they thought would be pleasing or gratifying to us. We went with them to Castle-Garden to see the fireworks, which was quite an agreeable entertainment—but to the *whites* who witnessed it, less *magnificent* than the sight of one of our large *prairies* would be when on fire.

We visited all the public buildings and places of amusement, which to us were truly astonishing, yet very gratifying.

Every body treated us with friendship, and many with great liberality. The squaws presented us many handsome little presents, that are said to be valuable. They were very kind, very good, and very pretty—for *pale faces!*

Among the men who treated us with marked friendship, by the presentation of many valuable presents, I cannot omit to mention the name of my old friend Crooks, of the American Fur Company.[139] I have known him long, and have always found him to be a good chief—one who gives good advice, and treats our people right. I shall always be proud to recognize him as a friend, and glad to shake him by the hand.

Having seen all the wonders of this *big village*, and being anxious to return to our people, our guide started with us for our own country. On arriving at Albany, the people were so anxious to see us, that they crowded the street and wharves, where the steam boat landed, so much, that it was almost impossible for us to pass to the hotel which had been provided for our reception.

We remained here but a short time, and then started for Detroit. I had spent many pleasant days at this place; and anticipated, on my arrival, to meet many of my old friends—but in this I was disappointed. What could be the cause of this? Are they all dead? Or what has become of them? I did not see our old father there, who had always gave me good advice, and treated me with friendship.

139. Black Hawk's longtime friend was Ramsay Crooks of the American Fur Company.

After leaving Detroit, it was but a few days before we landed at Prairie du Chien. The war chief at the fort treated us very kindly, as did the people generally. I called on the father of the Winnebago [Gen. J. M. Street,] to whom I had surrendered myself after the battle at the Bad Axe, who received me very friendly. I told him that I had left my great *medicine bag* with his chiefs before I gave myself up; and now, that I was to enjoy my liberty again, I was anxious to get it, that I might hand it down to my nation unsullied.

He said it was safe; he had heard his chiefs speak of it, and would get it and send it to me. I hope he will not forget his promise, as the whites generally do—because I have always heard that he was a good man, and a good father—and made no promises that he did not fulfill.

Passing down the Mississippi, I discovered a large collection of people in the mining country, on the west side of the river, *and on the ground that we had given to our relation,* DUBUQUE, *a long time ago.* I was surprised at this, as I had understood from our Great Father, that the Mississippi was to be the dividing line between his red and white children, and that he did not wish *either* to *cross it.* I was much pleased with this talk, as I knew that it would be much better for both parties. I have since found the country much settled by the whites further down, and near to our people, on the west side of the river. I am very much afraid, that in a few years, they will begin to drive and abuse our people, as they have formerly done. I may not live to *see* it, but I feel certain that the day is not distant.

When we arrived at Rock Island, Ke-o-kuck and the other chiefs were sent for. They arrived the next day with a great number of their young men, and came over to see me. I was pleased to see them, and they all appeared glad to see me. Among them were some who had lost relations during the war the year before. When we met, I perceived the tear of sorrow gush from their eyes at the recollection of their loss; yet they exhibited a smiling countenance, from the joy they felt at seeing me alive and well.

The next morning the war chief, our guide, convened a council at fort Armstrong. Ke-o-kuck and his party went to the fort; but, in consequence of the war chief not having called for me to accompany him, I concluded that I would wait until I was sent for. Consequently the interpreter came, and said, "they were ready, and had been waiting for me to come to the fort." I told him I was ready, and would accompany him. On our arrival there, the council commenced. The war chief said that the object of this council was to deliver me up to Ke-o-kuck. He then read a paper, and *directed me to follow Ke-o-kuck's advice, and be governed by his counsel in all things!* In this speech he said much that was mortifying to my feelings, and I made an *indignant reply.*

I did not know what object the war chief had in making such a speech, or whether he intended what he said; but I do know, that it was uncalled for, and did not become him. I have addressed many war chiefs, and have listened to their speeches with pleasure—but never had my feelings of pride and honor insulted on any former occasion. I am sorry that I was so hasty in reply to this chief, because I said that which I did not intend.

In this council, I met my old friend, a great war chief [Col. Wm. DAVENPORT,] whom I had known about eighteen years. He is a good and brave chief. He always treated me well, and gave me good advice. He made a speech to me on this occasion, very different from that of the other chief. It sounded like coming from a *brave!* He said he had known me a long time—that we had been good friends during that acquaintance—and, although he had fought against my braves, in our late war, he still extended the hand of friendship to me—and hoped, that I was now satisfied, from what I had seen in my travels, that it was folly to think of going to war against the whites, and would ever remain at peace. He said he would be glad to see me at all times—and on all occasions would be happy to give me good advice.

If our Great Father were to make such men our agents, he would much better subserve the interests of *our* people, as well as *his own*, than in any other way. The war chiefs all know our people, and are respected by them. If the war chiefs, at the different military posts on the frontiers, were made agents, they could always prevent difficulties from arising among the Indians and whites; and I have no doubt, had the war chief above alluded to, been our agent, we never would have had the difficulties with the whites which we have had. Our agents ought always to be *braves!* I would, therefore, recommend to our Great Father, the propriety of breaking up the present Indian establishment, and creating a new one—and of making the commanding officers, at the different frontier posts, the agents of the government for the different nations of Indians.

I have a good opinion of the American war chiefs, generally, with whom I am acquainted; and my people, who had an opportunity of seeing and becoming well acquainted with the great war chief [Gen. Winfield Scott], who made the last treaty with them, in conjunction with the great chief of Illinois [Governor Reynolds] all tell me that he is the *greatest brave* they ever saw, and a good man—one who fulfils all his promises. Our braves speak more highly of him, than any chief that has ever been among us, or made treaties with us. Whatever he says, may be depended upon. If he had been our Great Father, we never would have been *compelled* to join the British in their last war with America—and I have thought that, as our Great Father is changed every four years, that his children would do well to put this great war chief in his place—as they cannot find a better chief for a Great Father any where.

I would be glad if the *village criers* [editors,] in all the villages I passed through, would let their people know my wishes and opinions about this great war chief.

During my travels, my opinions were asked on different subjects—but for want of a good interpreter, were very seldom given. Presuming that they would be equally acceptable now, I have thought it a part of my duty, to lay the most important before the public.

The subject of colonizing the *negroes* was introduced, and my opinion asked, as to the best method of getting clear of these people.[140] I was not prepared, at the time, to answer—as I knew but little about their situation. I have since made many inquiries on the subject—and find that a number of states admit no slaves, whilst the balance hold these negroes as slaves, and are anxious, but do not know, how to get clear of them. I will now give my plan, which, when understood, I hope will be adopted.

Let the free states remove all the *male* negroes within their limits, to the slave states—then let our Great Father buy all the *female* negroes in the slave states, between the ages of twelve and twenty, and sell them to the people of the free states, for a term of years—say, those under fifteen, until they are twenty-one—and those of, and over fifteen, for five years—and continue to buy all the females

140. In 1832, slavery was a growing, intense issue discussed and debated in Northern states, which mostly advocated abolition while the Southern states advocated enslavement of Blacks.

in the slave states, as soon as they arrive at the age of twelve, and take them to the free states, and dispose of them in the same way as the first—and it will not be long before the country is clear of the *black skins,* about which, I am told, they have been talking, for a long time; and for which they have expended a large amount of money.

I have no doubt but our Great Father would willingly do his part in accomplishing this object for his children—as he could not lose much by it, and would make them all happy. If the free states did not want them all for servants, we would take the balance in our nation to help our women make corn.

I have not time now, nor is it necessary, to enter more into detail about my travels through the United States. The white people know all about them, and my people have started to their hunting grounds, and I am anxious to follow them.

Before I take leave of the public, I must contradict the story of some *village criers,* who (I have been told,) accuse me of "having murdered women and children among the whites!" This assertion is *false!* I never did, nor have I any knowledge that any of my nation ever killed a white women or child. I make this statement of truth, to satisfy the white people among whom I have been traveling, (and by whom I have been treated with great kindness,) that, when they shook me by the hand so cordially, they did not shake the hand that had ever been raised against any but warriors.

It has always been our custom to receive all strangers that come to our village or camps, in time of peace, on terms of friendship—to share with them the best provisions we have, and give them all the assistance in our power. If on a journey, or lost, to put them on the right trail, and if in want of mocasins [*sic*], to supply them. I feel grateful to the whites for the kind manner they treated me and my party whilst travelling among them—and from my heart I assure them, that the white man will always be welcome in our village or camps, as a brother. The tomahawk is buried forever! We will forget what has past [passed]—and may the watchword between the Americans and Sacs and Foxes, ever be—"*Friendship!*"[141]

I am now done. A few more moons and I must follow my fathers to the shades! May the Great Spirit keep our people and the whites always at peace—is the sincere wish of

BLACK HAWK

141. The most common phrase of the 374 US-Indian treaties is "peace and friendship." Donald L. Fixico, ed., *Indian Treaties in the United States: An Encyclopedia and Documents Collection* (ABC-CLIO, 2018), xvi.

SUGGESTED READING

A variety of readings describe the life of Black Hawk in distinct ways: leadership, Native patriotism, and frontier history. These books can be found in children's literature, biographies, tribal histories, regional histories, as well as Black Hawk's autobiography itself.

The earliest children's book about Black Hawk was published in 1943 by the Wheeler Publishing Company: Frank Lee Beals's *Chief Black Hawk.* It appeared in The American Adventure Series for middle and high school students. *The Story of the Black Hawk War* by Jim Hargrove and Ralph Canaday (Children's Press, 1986), describes the last major Indian war east of the Mississippi. A well-told story for those aged thirteen to eighteen is Arthur J. Beckhard's *Black Hawk* (The Good and the Beautiful, 2019).

Carole Marsh published *Black Hawk: Native American Leader* (Gallopade, 1998), a biographical story recommended for ages five to eleven (grades K–5). It engages young readers in reading activity programs found in schools and libraries. Carol March McLernon wrote the boyhood story of Black Hawk in *Black Hawk: A Boy and His Vision* in 2011 (Mirror Publishing). McLernon tells about Native life in the woods, hunting for beavers, and how Black Hawk left his village to seek a vision that led to his new name, Black Sparrow Hawk. For young adults, see John P. Bowes, *Black Hawk and the War of 1832* (Chelsea House Publishing, 2007).

The autobiography of Black Hawk that first appeared in print, edited by John Barton Patterson in 1833 has been reproduced: by J. B. Patterson, ed. (Continental Printing Company, 1882); Milo Milton Quaife (R. R. Donnelley & Sons Company, 1916); Donald Jackson (University of Illinois Press, 1955); Roger Nichols (Iowa State University Press, 1999); J. Gerald Kennedy (Penguin Classics, 2008); C. Wade Naney (CreateSpace Independent Publishing Platform, 2012); and Michael A. Lofaro (University of Tennessee Press, 2021). The autobiography has also been published as *Black Hawk's War, 1832: The Campaign against the Sauk & Fox Indians,* edited by Frank Everett Stevens (Leonaur Ltd, 2018). See also Carl Benn, *Native Memoirs from the War of 1812: Black Hawk and William Apess* (Johns Hopkins University Press, 2014).

Black Hawk's autobiography and how it was presented by Patterson has produced interesting conversations. For example, Neil Schmitz's "Captive Utterance: Black Hawk and Indian Irony," *Arizona Quarterly* 48, vol. 4 (Winter 1992), 1–18, and Timothy Sweet's "Masculinity in the Life of Black Hawk," *American Literature* 65, vol. 3 (September 1993), 475–99, suggest that Black Hawk manipulated the narrative to defend his cause and blames Americans for the war. Mark Wallace, in "Black Hawk's Autobiography: The Production and Use of an 'Indian' Voice," *American Indian Quarterly* 18, vol. 4 (Fall 1994), 481–94, suggests that as editor, Patterson controlled the process, and permitted Sauk ideas and feelings to come through as he wanted them to. The challenge of Black Hawk's leadership by Fox leader Keokuk, is told in Donald L. Fixico's "The Black Hawk-Keokuk Controversy," in *Indian Leaders, Oklahoma's First Statesmen,* H. Glen Jordan and Thomas M. Holm, eds.(Oklahoma Historical Society, 1979), 64–78.

A biography of Black Hawk is Roger L. Nichols's *Black Hawk and the Warrior's Path* (Harlan Davidson, Inc., 1992). There is also Kerry A. Trask's biography *Black Hawk: The Battle for the Heart of America* (Holt Paperbacks, 2007). An engaging narrative, this book is more than a biography and tells the frontier story of struggle from the view of Black Hawk and his people. Readers of novels will appreciate the early historical work by Cyrenus Cole, *I Am a Man: The Indian Black Hawk* (State Historical Society of Iowa, 1938).

For readers who might be interested in the personal views of those involved in the Black Hawk War, see, Crawford B. Thayer, *Hunting a Shadow: The Search for Black Hawk: An Eye-Witness Account of the Black Hawk War of 1832* (Banta Press, 1981). See also Patrick J. Jung, *The Black Hawk War of 1832* (University of Oklahoma Press, 2007). Routes on maps and personal views in 1832 might interest some readers in Ben Strand's *Black Hawk War Guide: Landmarks, Battlefields, Museums & Firsthand Accounts* (The History Press, 2021). A similar volume of interest is Nicholas A. Brown's and Sarah E. Kanouse's *Re-Collecting Black Hawk: Landscape, Memory, and Power in the American Midwest* (University of Pittsburgh Press, 2015.)

The war itself is the focus of *Indian America: The Black Hawk War* by Miriam Gurko (Crowell, 1970). See also Perry A. Armstrong, *The Sauks and the Black Hawk War: With Biographical sketches, etc.* (H.W. Rokker, printer, 1887) and John A. Wakefield, *History of the Black Hawk War* (The Caxton Club, 1908). Reuben Thwaites, *The Story of the Black Hawk War* originally published in 1892 was reissued in 2023 by Legare Street Press. See also, Cecil D. Eby, *"That Disgraceful Affair": The Black Hawk War* (W. W. Norton, 1973); Benjamin Drake, *The Life and Adventures of Black Hawk: With Sketches of Keokuk, the Sauk and Fox Indians, and the Late Black Hawk War* (Forgotten Books, 2018), and Benjamin Drake, *Great Indian Chief of the West Or, Life and Adventures of Black Hawk* (CreateSpace Independent Publishing Platform, 2012). Other Indian nations involved in the war and their roles are described in John W. Hall's *Uncommon Defense: Indian Allies in the Black Hawk War* (Harvard University Press, 2009). (The Black Hawk War of 1832 should not be confused with the Black Hawk War of Utah that occurred in 1849 and lingered until 1873.) The influence of Black Hawk and his patriotism in leading a portion of his people to reclaim their homeland inspired a lengthy poem that appeared in Elbert J. Smith's *Ma-Ka-Tai-Me-She-Kia-Kiak: or, Black Hawk and Scenes in the West, A National Poem: In Six Cantos* (Edward Kearny, 1848).

Readers who are interested in the tribal history of the Sauk and Fox, also known as the Mesquakie, will appreciate the early volume of William T. Hagan, *The Sac and Fox Indians* (University of Oklahoma Press, 1958). A general tribal history for young readers is Theresa Lacey's and Nancy Bonvillain's *The Sac and Fox* (Chelsea House Publishers, 1995). More specifically on society, culture, and war see Charles Callender, "Sauk," in *Handbook of North American Indians: Northeast,* vol. 15, ed. Bruce Trigger (Smithsonian Institution, 1987), 648–55, and Charles Callender, "Fox," in *Handbook of North American Indians: Northeast,* vol. 15, ed. Bruce Trigger (Smithsonian Institution,

1987), 636–47. An early important work about the cultures of the Sauk and Fox is Thomas Forsyth's *An Account of the Manners and Customs of the Sauk and Fox Nations of Indians* (A. H. Clark Company, 1912). An early work on Fox culture is William Jones's *Ethnography of the Fox Indians,* Bureau of American Ethnology, *Bulletin No. 125* (Smithsonian Institution, 1939).

The three Sac and Fox tribes offer online sources and helpful information: Sac and Fox Nation of Missouri in Kansas and Nebraska, Reserve, Kansas, https://www.sacandfoxks.com; Sac and Fox Tribes of the Mississippi in Iowa, Tama, Iowa, https://www.meskwaki.org; and Sac and Fox Nation of Oklahoma, Stroud, Oklahoma, https://www.sacandfoxnation-nsn.gov.

INDEX